complete colour mixing guide

a visual reference to mixing acrylic KU-326-322 colours

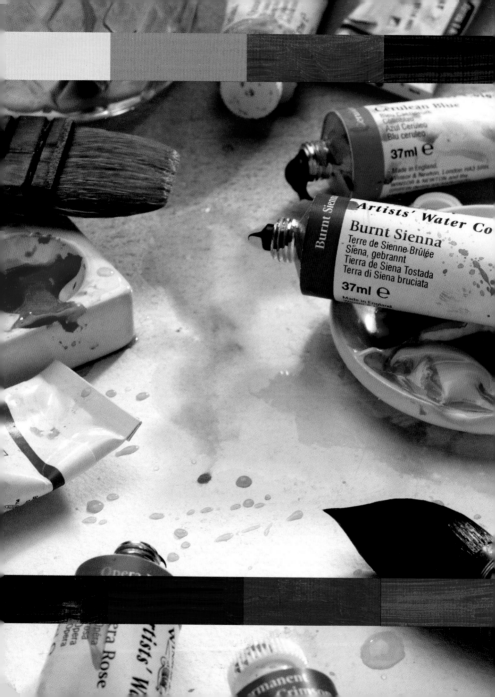

complete colour mixing guide

a visual reference to mixing acrylics, oils and watercolours

JOHN BARBER

Search Press

First published in Great Britain in 2010 by
Search Press Limited
Wellwood, North Farm Road
Tunbridge Wells
Kent TN2 3DR

Conceived and created by
Axis Publishing Limited
8c Accommodation Road
London NW11 8ED
www.axispublishing.co.uk

Creative Director: Siân Keogh
Designer: Sean Keogh
Project Editor: Anna Southgate
Production Manager: Bili Books

ISBN 978-1-84448-622-9

Printed in China

9 8 7 6 5 4 3 2 1

contents

introduction

Watercolour as a medium developed from topographical drawings worked in monochrome grey or brown ink. Although several artists emerged to produce works in the medium during the 18th century, it was J.M.W. Turner (1775–1851) who developed watercolour into a serious competitor to oil painting through his choice and use of colour. Today watercolour is the medium of choice for thousands of painters working in a variety of styles and a broad range of subjects.

Acrylics are readily mixed with water, but once they are dry, they are inert, flexible and do not become brittle. They can be applied in any manner from thin liquid washes to solid chunks of paint built up with the palette knife. Acrylics dry within a few hours, a quality that eliminates the problems of dust and cracking encountered with oil paints. Because these polymer resins are inert and, once dry, do not seep, many materials such as sand, metallic dust or glass can be used to widen the possible range of effects in both craft work and picture making.

Oil paints are made by mixing pigments with drying oils, usually linseed or safflower oil, although artists use many other oils to obtain particular handling qualities. The slow drying qualities of the oil medium enable the paint to be manipulated over long periods, allowing passages of painting to be removed or altered over several days. This does make the handling of freshly painted work difficult and makes the medium unpopular with holiday painters and travellers. For these artists who wish to paint in an opaque manner, acrylics or simply adding white paint (gouache) to water colours are frequently used alternatives.

ABOUT THIS BOOK

This book on colour mixing is intended for both amateur and professional artists, and should prove invaluable both in the studio and when out painting on location. You can use it to precisely match any shade you want to reproduce in your work. The 25 colours chosen for the colour wheels give a comprehensive range of 2,400 two-colour mixes. The selected colours have been chosen as the most useful for a wide range of painting. All the colours can be located in the colour charts and matched by mixing only the two colours shown. This innovative method has the great advantage of enabling you to mix the chosen colour with the absolute minimum number of colours, thereby obtaining the cleanest and brightest tints possible. The need to add a third or even a fourth colour when attempting to match a colour is avoided. (Generally, the more colours you mix together, the greater the tendency to produce a dull finished colour.)

Each pair of colours is shown in five degrees of a mixture, and on each colour wheel percentages are marked as a guide to the proportion of each colour that was used to produce the mix. Start with one colour at full strength, and then add the second colour gradually until the desired colour on the wheel is matched. Note that these mixes were made using one manufacturer's paints; colours by other manufacturers will give varying results.

CHOICE OF COLOURS

It may seem surprising that several lovely subtle colours are not included. However, by looking at the appropriate colour wheels, you will find very close matches to most shades. Experienced painters may find that some of their favourite colours are missing from the charts, but may be surprised by how many can be replicated extremely closely by other two-colour combinations.

MIXING COLOUR

When mixing colours, start with the lighter colour and gradually add the darker colour to it. In this way, you will avoid mixing too much paint. If you start with too much of the darker or stronger colour, you will need a great deal of the lighter colour to create the tint you are trying to achieve.

how to use this book

Each two-page spread features a named colour from the ranges below. In practice, most artists will use far fewer colours than this. Colour mixtures are added to each base colour in different percentage strengths, which will help you achieve the precise shade you want. The colours are organized into colour groups: yellows, reds, purples, blues, greens, and browns, with mix colours chosen as being of most use to artists working in watercolours, acrylics and oils. The hue variations information at the foot of each two-page spread shows you where to look if your mix is not quite what you want.

WATERCOLOUR PALETTE

lemon yellow
cadmium yellow light
cadmium yellow
quinacridone gold
raw sienna
burnt sienna
cadmium red
cadmium red deep
permanent rose
opera rose
perylene violet
permanent mauve
violet
French ultramarine
cobalt blue
cerulean blue (green shade)
Prussian blue
phthalo turquoise
viridian
permanent sap green
olive green
raw umber
burnt umber
sepia
Payne's gray

ACRYLIC PALETTE

lemon yellow
cadmium yellow medium
azo yellow medium
cadmium orange
cadmium red light
naphthol red light
quinacridone red
permanent rose
permanent alizarin crimson
quinacridone violet
dioxazine purple
ultramarine blue
cobalt blue
phthalo blue green shade
cerulean blue hue
phthalo turquoise
phthalo green blue shade
permanent sap green
olive green
yellow ochre
burnt sienna
red iron oxide
quinacridone burnt orange
raw umber
Payne's gray

OIL PALETTE

lemon yellow
cadmium yellow pale
Naples yellow deep
cadmium yellow deep
orange
cadmium scarlet
cadmium red deep
permanent rose
permanent alizarin crimson
quinacridone magenta
violet (dioxazine)
cobalt blue
cerulean blue (red shade)
French ultramarine
indanthrene blue
manganese blue hue
phthalo turquoise
cobalt turquoise
cadmium green pale
emerald green
viridian
Prussian green
burnt sienna
light red
raw umber

Use the at-a-glance percentage mixes to see what will result from a mix of two colours in a range of five different percentage strengths. The colour at the centre of the "wheel" is 100 per cent of the colour named on the spread; the outer ends of the "spokes" are 100 per cent strength of the mixer colour.

section colour: Colours are grouped into primary or secondary colours; related colours appear one after the other.

percentage mix The percentages of each colour are indicated, from full-strength main shade at the centre to full-strength second colour at the edge.

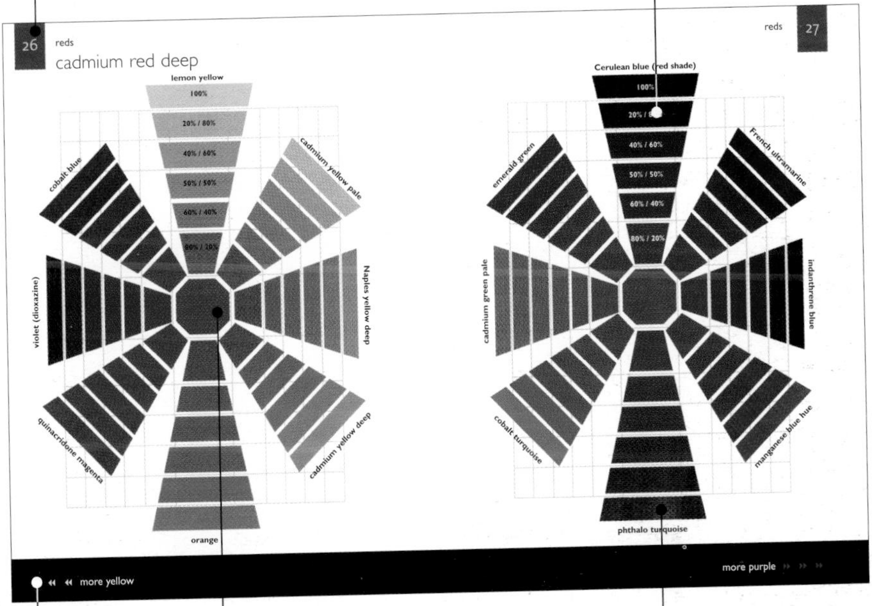

26 reds
cadmium red deep

lemon yellow
100%
20% / 80%
40% / 60%
50% / 50%
60% / 40%
80% / 20%

cobalt blue

cadmium yellow pale

violet (dioxazine)

Naples yellow deep

quinacridone magenta

cadmium yellow deep

orange

⬤ ◄◄ ◄◄ more yellow

reds 27

Cerulean blue (red shade)
100%
20% / 80%
40% / 60%
50% / 50%
60% / 40%
80% / 20%

emerald green

French ultramarine

cadmium green pale

indanthrene blue

cobalt turquoise

manganese blue hue

phthalo turquoise

more purple ►► ►► ►►

hue variations If your mix is not right, going back in the selector will give mixes containing more of a different colour.

base colour One of the 25 colours shown opposite appears on every spread, with mixes of percentages of further colours.

mix colour Full strength swatches of the mixer colour appear at the ends of the spokes of the colour wheel.

understanding colour

An understanding of the basics of colour theory and the colour wheel is very important for every artist. It can help you realize endless creative possibilities for your work. Colour, after all, is one of the fundamental tools of painting and armed with the knowledge of how to use their harmonies, contrasts and characteristics will help add excitement and dynamism to the paintings you produce.

the colour wheel

Successful painting often depends as much on the effects created by your colour choice as on composition, which is where an understanding of how colour works comes in.

The colour wheel is a great reference for artists. The three colours in the centre are the primary colours. Primary colours are the ones that cannot be obtained by mixing other colours together. The middle ring shows the colours that are created when you mix two of the primaries. Red and yellow make orange; blue and yellow make green; blue and red make purple. These are called secondary colours, and show the colours you can expect to create when you mix primary watercolours in your palette. All colours can, in theory, be created by mixing varying amounts of the primaries. The outer ring breaks down the secondary colours further into 12 shades.

For each picture you paint, you will need a colour to represent each of the primary colours so that by mixing them, you can obtain all the secondary colours. The primary colours you choose should be determined by the scene you wish to paint. For example, if you are painting cool, clear skies and distant hills, choose cobalt blue to represent blue in the colour wheel, permanent rose to represent red, and cadmium lemon to represent yellow. All three colours are cool, enabling you to maintain a consistently cool palette – no clashing "hot" colours will appear. Likewise, when painting a warm scene, use warm blue, red, and yellow colours for your primaries. This idea, along with using

complementary colours, which appear opposite each other on the colour wheel and produce harmonious contrasts, help you keep your colours balanced.

A good exercise is to make colour wheels for warm and cool colours. Draw several circles 4 inches (10 cm) in diameter and divide each circle into six pie slices. Paint your three primaries in alternate slices and then mix them: red with yellow for orange, blue with yellow for green, and blue with red for purple. Place these secondary colours in between the primaries and you will see exactly which ones work out well for your picture.

COLOUR TERMS

HUE
Hue indicates the strength of a colour from full saturation down to white. In practical terms, if you buy any colour labelled "hue" it means that the colour is less than full strength. This is used as a way of reducing the cost of expensive pigments.

TONE
Tone is the degree of darkness from black to white that creates shade and light. For example, in a black-and-white photograph you can see and understand any object independently of colour, solely by its graduation from light to dark. The word "shade" is often used instead of "tone".

COLOUR
Colour results from the division of light into separate wavelengths, creating the visible spectrum. Our brains interpret each wavelength as a different colour. The colour wheel is an aid that helps us understand how colours are arranged in relation to each other.

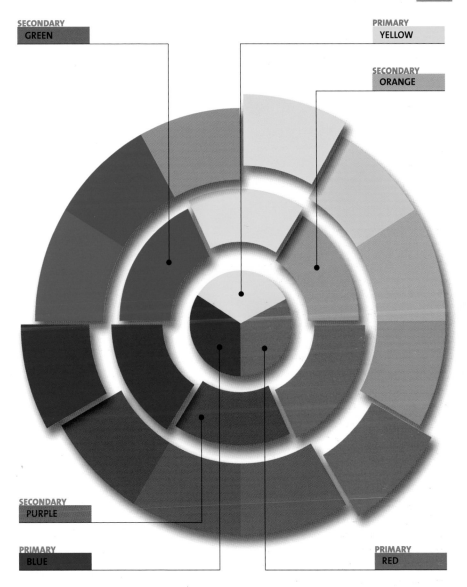

SECONDARY
GREEN

PRIMARY
YELLOW

SECONDARY
ORANGE

SECONDARY
PURPLE

PRIMARY
BLUE

PRIMARY
RED

the colour wheel

COMPLEMENTARY COLOUR

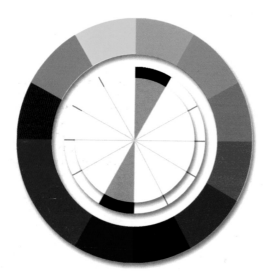

The colours that are opposite each other on the colour wheel are called complementary colours. These work together to create a harmonious reaction. Try using them side-by-side in your work – they will each appear to be stronger by contrast, bouncing off of each other.

TRIADIC COLOUR

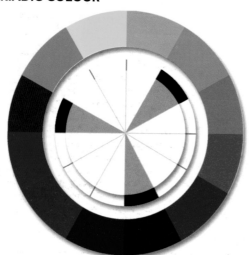

Triadic colour occurs when a "chord" of three colours is used in combination. A mixture of any two colours of the triad used next to a third, unmixed colour will give many different effects. A triad of colours from any part of the wheel is the basis for a good colour composition.

SPLIT COMPLEMENTARY COLOUR

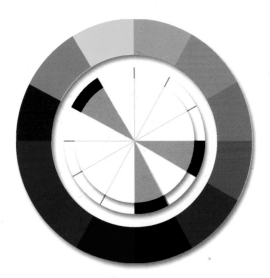

Split complementaries create three colours: the first colour, chosen from any point on the wheel, plus the two colours that come on either side of the first colour's natural complementary colour. These three colours will give plenty of unexpected colour schemes.

INDOOR/OUTDOOR TEST

The indoor/outdoor test is designed to show the effect that artificial or subdued lighting has on colours when compared with daylight. If you look at the four strips indoors, you can see hardly any difference between the colours on the right and the ones on the left. Step out into the daylight and you will be able to see that the right-hand side is noticeably darker. This sort of phenomenon plays an important part in how we perceive colour, and all artists have to be aware of it. Although it is never quite as obvious as in the experiment, it does help to explain why art studios are built with high skylights, ideally facing north. For artists whose pictures depend on great colour accuracy, good daylight is essential.

watercolour harmonies

This sketch of the coast of Ireland, with its sparkling waves and fleecy clouds, was painted with a narrow palette of cool blues and greys that suggest pale sunlight and the distance of the coastline. It was created with just three colours – cobalt blue (blue is the coolest colour on the colour wheel), Payne's gray, and yellow.

This winter scene is created around four colours – cobalt blue, Hooker's green, Payne's gray, and burnt sienna. The most important element is the cool grey background, which establishes that this is a misty day. The dark trees make a series of verticals that create the stillness of the scene. The clever use of burnt sienna makes the other colours look even cooler.

This is a richly painted still life, with warm oranges, reds, and yellows in the flowers, a wide range of greens in the leaves, and a solid rectangle of deep blue in the watering can. The pink wash over the table and far wall brings in purple shades. The blue colour of the can is taken up into the background leaves to make a soft, turquoise green. This vibrant still life uses most of the colours of the colour wheel to create an overall feeling of warmth.

acrylic harmonies

The atmosphere of this picture is created by the all-pervading red of the underpainting. Even the greens and blues are brought back toward the warm end of the spectrum, with all sorts of subtle purples holding the harmonies of colour together to beautifully evoke a mysterious Parisian twilight.

This detailed scene contains a wealth of texture and modelling, but the dominant colour note is the cool grey of the cock bird's back. In combination with the bright yellow greens and the blue grey of the rocks, it hardly leaves the cool blue end of the palette, except for the blush of sienna on the bird's throat.

The woodland trees in winter filter the weak sunlight into patches on the forest path. A dominant motif of thin vertical lines gives the picture a feeling of repose, and the blurring of the trunks by the low sun adds the element of infinity.

Ultramarine and raw umber keep all the tints cool, and weak yellow ochre warms the snow colour where the sun penetrates the mist. This painting amply demonstrates the value of using only a restricted palette of colours in some of your works.

oil colour harmonies

The yellow-green-blue range from the colour wheel saturates the scene and it is the bright, almost pure cadmium lemon spots that add the sparkle and interest. The appearance of the burnt sienna in the foreground accentuates the greens.

These barges on the Thames below Westminster Bridge act as a foil to the sparkling water painted in a range of closely related cool colours, with hints of the sun's warmth in the pinks. Here the violet and permanent rose from the colour wheel provide a range of tints for the reflections that influence the colour temperature throughout the picture.

The Wildstrübel, which translates as "tousled head" because the mountain always seems to have a wreath of clouds around its peak, was painted from a mountain house across the valley. In contrast to the Thames painting, the light and air are crystal clear and the whole range of blues and violets crisp and defined in clear patches. The clouds rising from the valley floor were scumbled on after the rest of the picture was dry, a technique often needed in this sort of oil painting to avoid blurring existing details.

watercolour mixes

The following pages feature 25 main watercolours that are the most popular with amateur and professional artists. The mixes provide excellent evidence of how few colours a painter actually needs to produce bright, vibrant colours. Use these mixes as guides to help you achieve the exact shade you want, whatever your subject.

papers and brushes

Watercolour painting requires very little equipment: pan or tube paints, sable or synthetic brushes, good paper, and clean water. In watercolour, fine pigments produce clear, bright washes that can be modified by the slightest amount of other colours. This gives the medium great subtlety and flexibility, but if the water in your jar is tinted, then all your colours are being mixed with that tint, however pale it is. It may not be particularly noticeable to you, but it is happening. The ideal solution is to use two large clear jars so that you can see how much the water is coloured, using one to wash your brushes and the other to add water to your colours. In practice, most artists use only one jar, particularly when painting outdoors, and change the water frequently.

To ensure the greatest colour accuracy, all the colour patches in this book were mixed with clean boiled water and a brush washed under the tap when each patch was finished, until the water ran clear.

WATERCOLOUR PAPERS

The paper you choose will have a great influence on the way your paints work, and it is advisable to try a selection before investing in large pads of one type of paper. The surface preferred by many artists is a good-quality rough (or "Not") watercolour paper, but much fine work has been done on papers and boards that were not originally intended as a painting surface. Tinted papers can also be used. On these the contrast between colours will be weaker, as every transparent wash will show some of the paper's own colour through it. J.M.W. Turner used many types of paper, including writing papers, and had slate-grey paper bound into sketchbooks for his Venice studies. To counter the darkness of the paper, he added white to his lighter tones. This is now standard practice with artists working on tinted papers. Most of the papers in his sketchbooks had quite smooth surfaces.

BRUSHES

The range of brushes now available is enormous. Pure sable brushes are the highest quality, but expensive; combinations of synthetics and sable offer superior quality at an affordable price. A good starting set of brushes for most needs includes pointed sable brushes up to size 14 for tight control and accuracy; a couple of riggers for drawing long continuous lines (these can be synthetic or sable); broad, flat synthetic wash brushes, 1 cm, 2.5 cm and 5 cm (½ inch, 1 inch, 2 inches); and a mop brush of squirrel hair for wetting the paper and brushing in large areas.

Try out a lot of different paper textures to find out which best suits your style of work. Paint patches of different colours on different surfaces to see how they react.

the watercolour palettes

The colours below are the most popular watercolours with professional and amateur artists. They are all available in art stores and via the Internet. Colours included in many preselected paint boxes are also chosen from this range.

lemon yellow
benzimidazolone

cadmium yellow light
benzimidazolone

cadmium yellow
cadmium zinc sulphide,
cadmium sulphoselenide

quinacridone gold
quinacridones, nickel azo

raw sienna
transparent synthetic
iron oxides

burnt sienna
transparent synthetic
iron oxide

cadmium red
cadmium sulphoselenide

cadmium red deep
pyrrole

permanent rose
quinacridone

opera rose
fluorescent dye/resin-based
pigment, quinacridone

perylene violet
perylene

permanent mauve
manganese phosphate

violet
carbozole dioxazine

French ultramarine
complex sodium aluminium
silicate containing sulphur

cobalt blue
cobalt aluminate

cerulean blue
cobalt stannate

Prussian blue
alkali ferriferrocyanide

phthalo turquoise
copper-free phthalocyanine

viridian
hydrated chromium oxide

permanent sap green
brominated copper
phthalocyanine, isoindolinone

olive green
synthetic iron oxide, chlorinated
copper phthalocyanine

raw umber
natural iron oxide

burnt umber
natural and
synthetic iron oxides

sepia
carbon black,
synthetic iron oxide

Payne's gray
copper phthalocyanine, carbon
black, quinacridone

SUGGESTED PALETTES

It is a good idea for beginners to start with a very restricted palette of six colours and use the charts referring to these six colours to develop their colour skills and discover their preferences. They can then augment their palette as they gain experience. A good minimum palette for a beginner is shown here:

cadmium yellow light

cadmium red

French ultramarine

burnt sienna

viridian

violet

Brushes come in many shapes and sizes, but most of those suitable for watercolour are made from sable or other animal hair, or synthetics.

lemon yellow

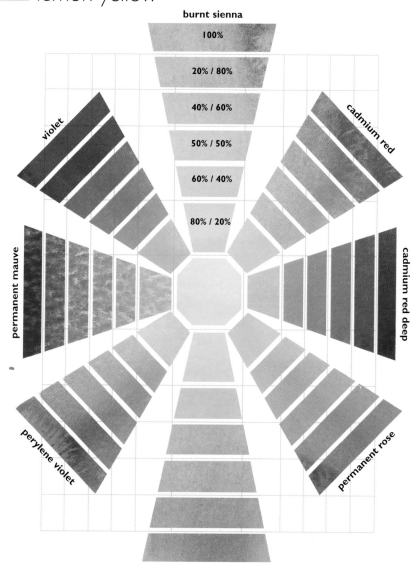

burnt sienna

100%

20% / 80%

40% / 60%

50% / 50%

60% / 40%

80% / 20%

violet

cadmium red

permanent mauve

cadmium red deep

perylene violet

permanent rose

opera rose

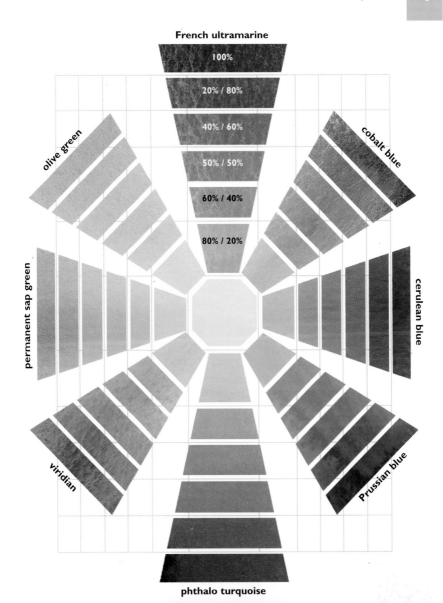

French ultramarine

100%

20% / 80%

40% / 60%

50% / 50%

60% / 40%

80% / 20%

olive green

cobalt blue

permanent sap green

cerulean blue

viridian

Prussian blue

phthalo turquoise

cadmium yellow light

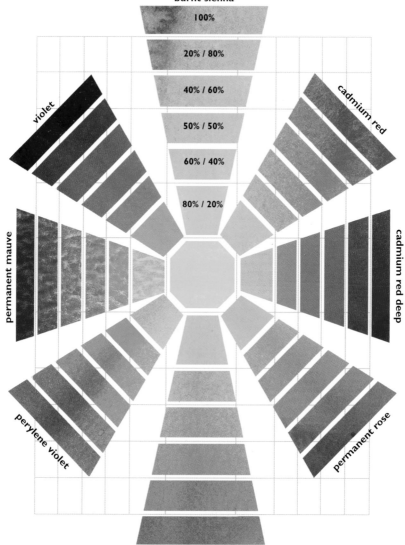

burnt sienna

100%

20% / 80%

40% / 60%

50% / 50%

60% / 40%

80% / 20%

violet

cadmium red

permanent mauve

cadmium red deep

perylene violet

permanent rose

opera rose

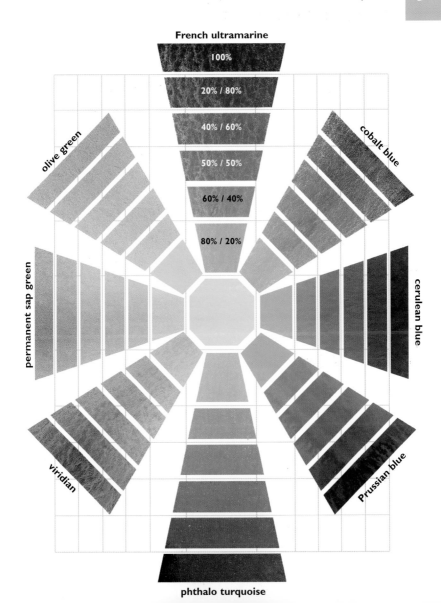

French ultramarine

100%

20% / 80%

40% / 60%

50% / 50%

60% / 40%

80% / 20%

olive green

cobalt blue

permanent sap green

cerulean blue

viridian

Prussian blue

phthalo turquoise

cadmium yellow

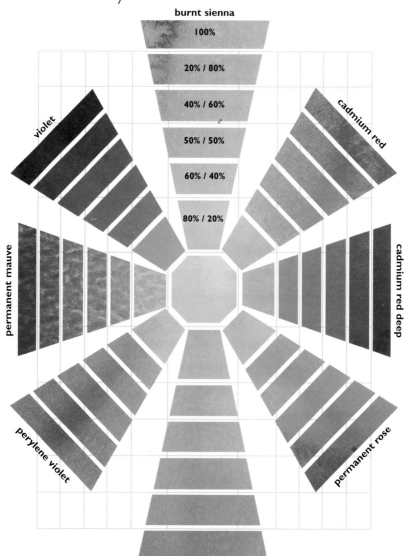

burnt sienna

100%

20% / 80%

40% / 60%

50% / 50%

60% / 40%

80% / 20%

violet

cadmium red

permanent mauve

cadmium red deep

perylene violet

permanent rose

opera rose

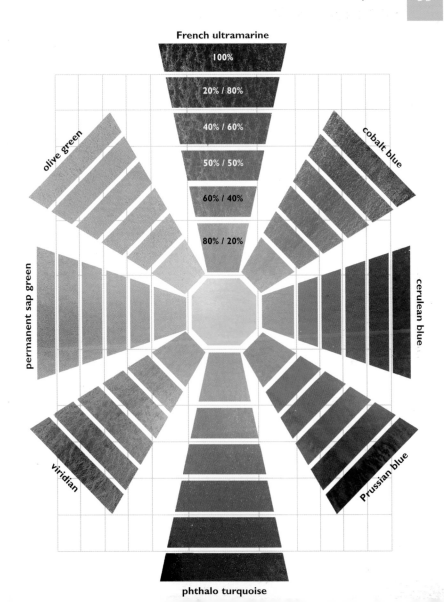

French ultramarine

100%

20% / 80%

40% / 60%

50% / 50%

60% / 40%

80% / 20%

olive green

cobalt blue

permanent sap green

cerulean blue

viridian

Prussian blue

phthalo turquoise

quinacridone gold

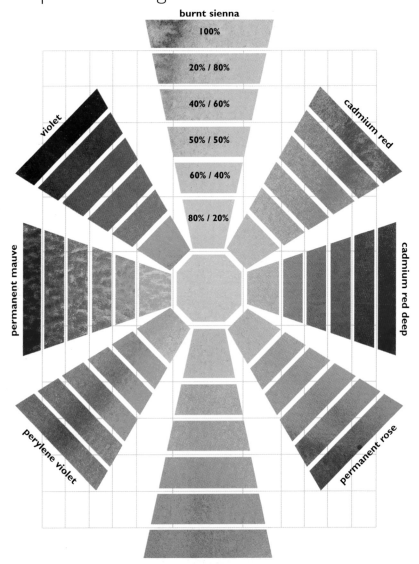

burnt sienna

100%

20% / 80%

40% / 60%

50% / 50%

60% / 40%

80% / 20%

violet

cadmium red

permanent mauve

cadmium red deep

perylene violet

permanent rose

opera rose

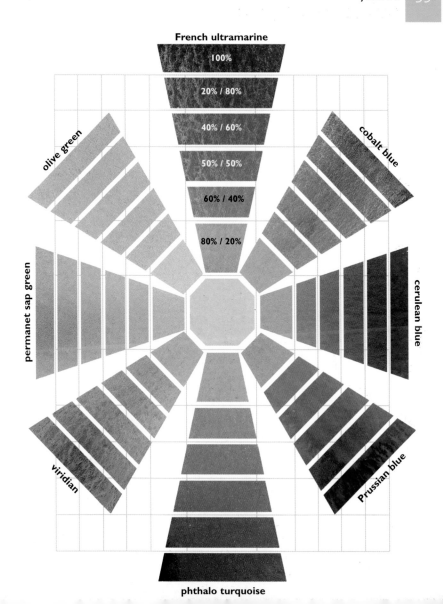

French ultramarine

100%

20% / 80%

40% / 60%

50% / 50%

60% / 40%

80% / 20%

olive green

cobalt blue

permanet sap green

cerulean blue

viridian

Prussian blue

phthalo turquoise

raw sienna

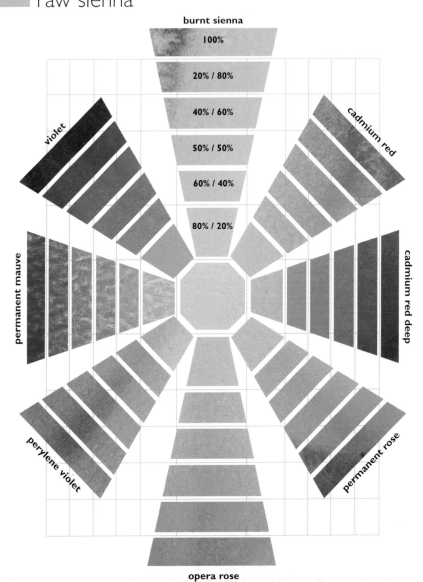

burnt sienna

100%

20% / 80%

40% / 60%

50% / 50%

60% / 40%

80% / 20%

violet

cadmium red

permanent mauve

cadmium red deep

perylene violet

permanent rose

opera rose

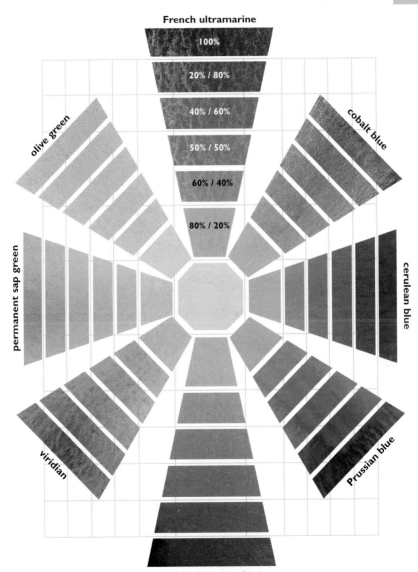

French ultramarine

100%

20% / 80%

40% / 60%

50% / 50%

60% / 40%

80% / 20%

olive green

cobalt blue

permanent sap green

cerulean blue

viridian

Prussian blue

phthalo turquoise

burnt sienna

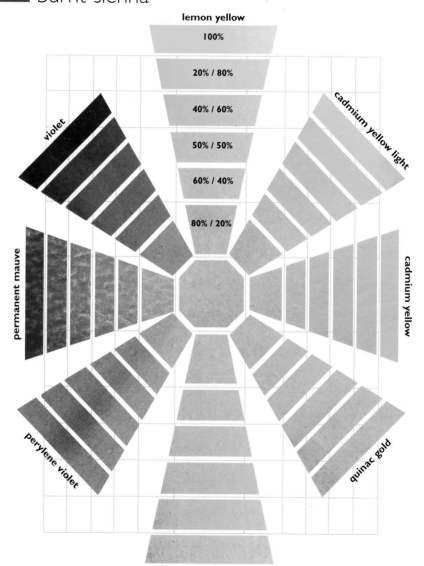

lemon yellow

100%

20% / 80%

40% / 60%

50% / 50%

60% / 40%

80% / 20%

violet

cadmium yellow light

permanent mauve

cadmium yellow

perylene violet

quinac gold

raw sienna

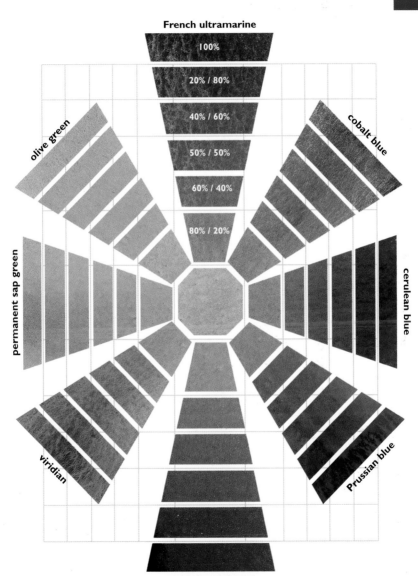

French ultramarine

100%

20% / 80%

40% / 60%

50% / 50%

60% / 40%

80% / 20%

cobalt blue

olive green

permanent sap green

cerulean blue

viridian

Prussian blue

phthalo turquoise

cadmium red

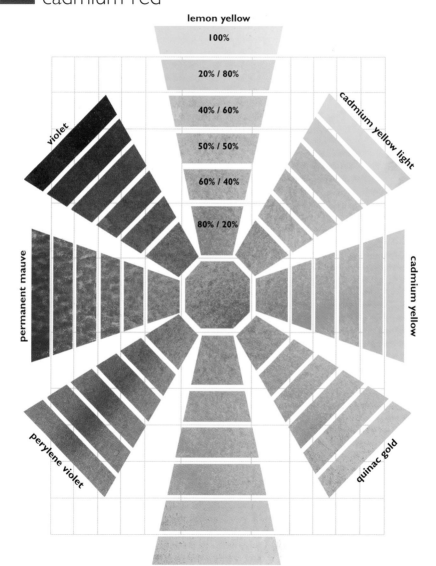

lemon yellow

100%

20% / 80%

40% / 60%

50% / 50%

60% / 40%

80% / 20%

violet

cadmium yellow light

permanent mauve

cadmium yellow

perylene violet

quinac gold

raw sienna

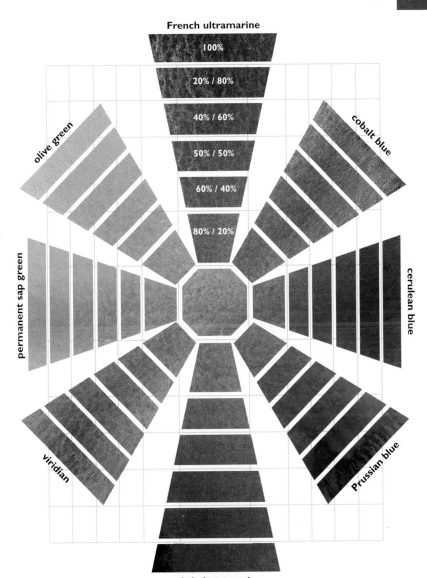

French ultramarine

100%

20% / 80%

40% / 60%

50% / 50%

60% / 40%

80% / 20%

olive green

cobalt blue

permanent sap green

cerulean blue

viridian

Prussian blue

phthalo turquoise

cadmium red deep

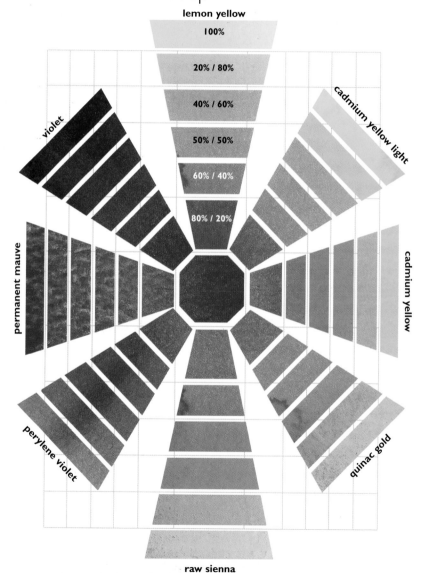

lemon yellow
100%
20% / 80%
40% / 60%
50% / 50%
60% / 40%
80% / 20%

violet

cadmium yellow light

permanent mauve

cadmium yellow

perylene violet

quinac gold

raw sienna

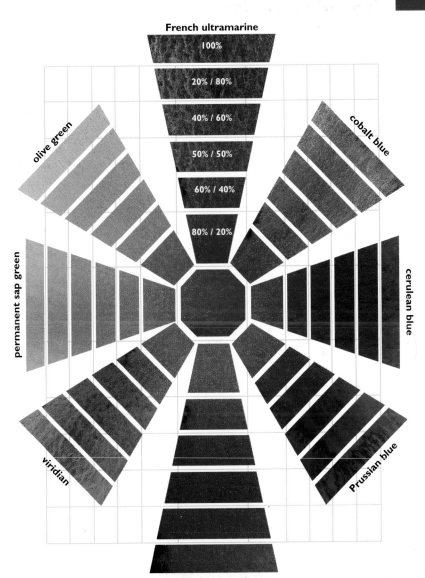

French ultramarine

100%

20% / 80%

40% / 60%

50% / 50%

60% / 40%

80% / 20%

olive green

cobalt blue

permanent sap green

cerulean blue

viridian

Prussian blue

phthalo turquoise

permanent rose

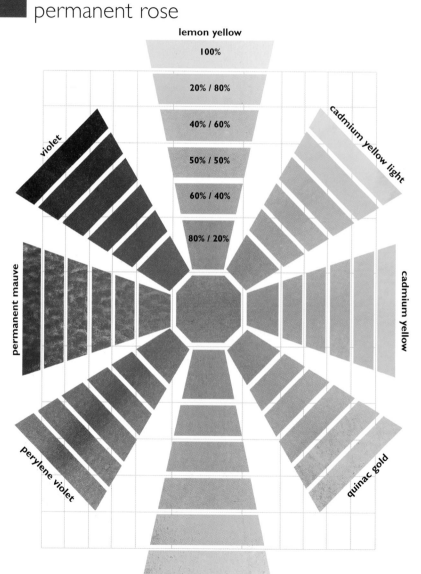

lemon yellow

100%

20% / 80%

40% / 60%

50% / 50%

60% / 40%

80% / 20%

violet

cadmium yellow light

permanent mauve

cadmium yellow

perylene violet

quinac gold

raw sienna

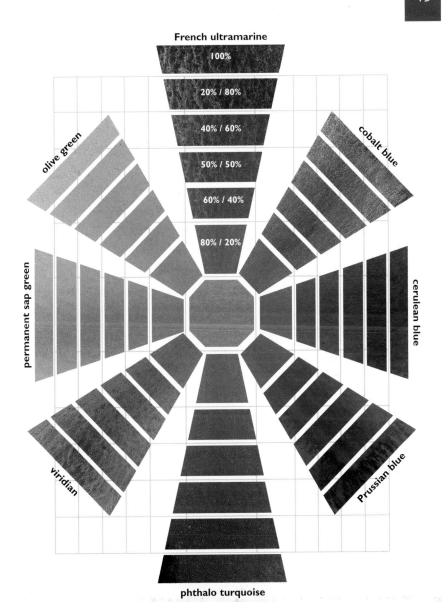

French ultramarine

100%

20% / 80%

40% / 60%

50% / 50%

60% / 40%

80% / 20%

olive green

cobalt blue

permanent sap green

cerulean blue

viridian

Prussian blue

phthalo turquoise

opera rose

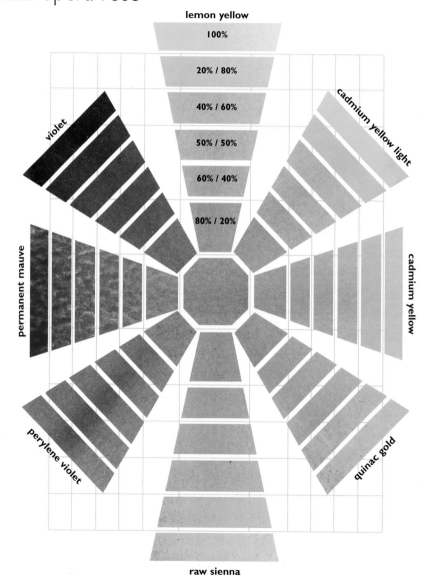

lemon yellow

100%

20% / 80%

40% / 60%

50% / 50%

60% / 40%

80% / 20%

violet

cadmium yellow light

permanent mauve

cadmium yellow

perylene violet

quinac gold

raw sienna

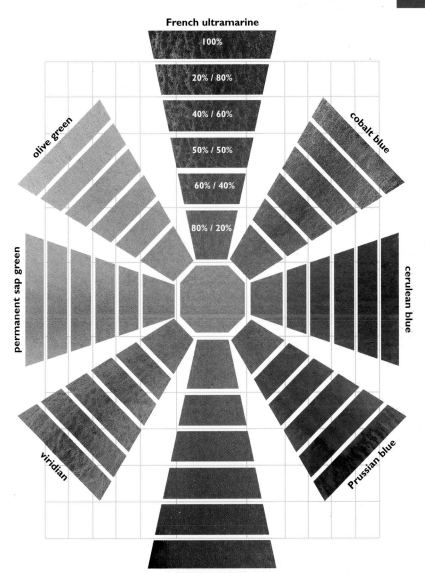

French ultramarine

100%

20% / 80%

40% / 60%

50% / 50%

60% / 40%

80% / 20%

olive green

cobalt blue

permanent sap green

cerulean blue

viridian

Prussian blue

phthalo turquoise

perylene violet

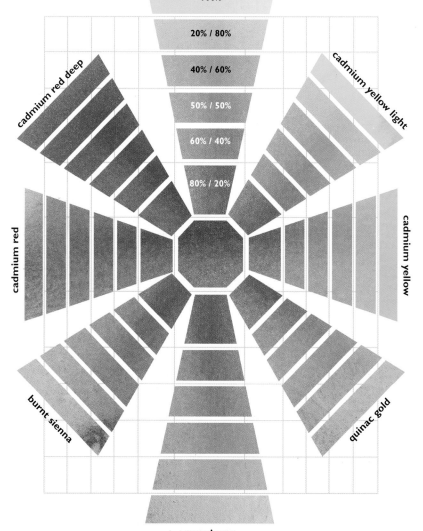

lemon yellow

100%

20% / 80%

40% / 60%

50% / 50%

60% / 40%

80% / 20%

cadmium red deep

cadmium yellow light

cadmium red

cadmium yellow

burnt sienna

quinac gold

raw sienna

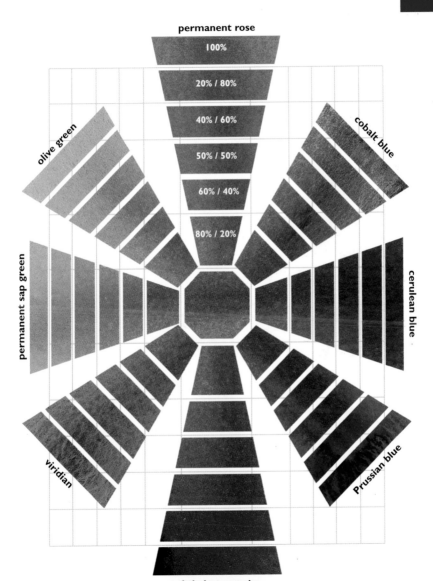

permanent rose

100%

20% / 80%

40% / 60%

50% / 50%

60% / 40%

80% / 20%

olive green

cobalt blue

permanent sap green

cerulean blue

viridian

Prussian blue

phthalo turquoise

permanent mauve

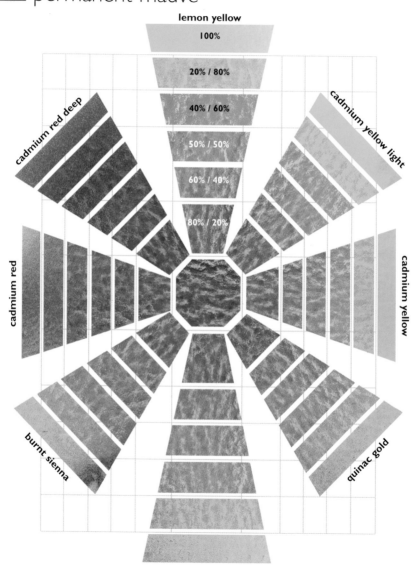

lemon yellow

100%

20% / 80%

40% / 60%

50% / 50%

60% / 40%

80% / 20%

cadmium red deep

cadmium yellow light

cadmium red

cadmium yellow

burnt sienna

quinac gold

raw sienna

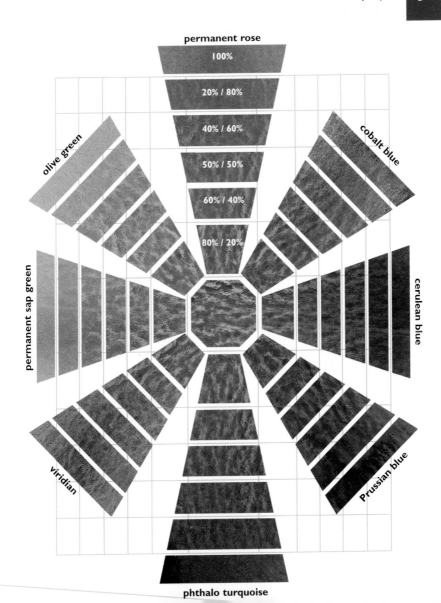

permanent rose

100%

20% / 80%

40% / 60%

50% / 50%

60% / 40%

80% / 20%

olive green

cobalt blue

permanent sap green

cerulean blue

viridian

Prussian blue

phthalo turquoise

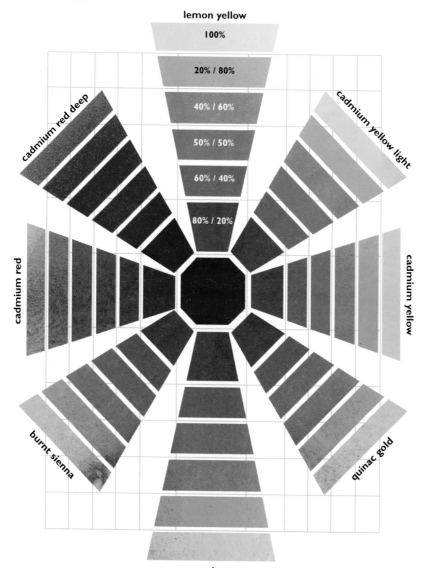

lemon yellow
100%
20% / 80%
40% / 60%
50% / 50%
60% / 40%
80% / 20%

cadmium red deep

cadmium yellow light

cadmium red

cadmium yellow

burnt sienna

quinac gold

raw sienna

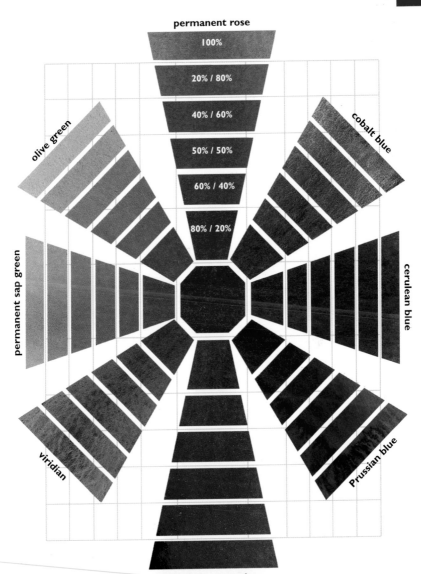

permanent rose

100%

20% / 80%

40% / 60%

50% / 50%

60% / 40%

80% / 20%

olive green

cobalt blue

permanent sap green

cerulean blue

viridian

Prussian blue

phthalo turquoise

French ultramarine

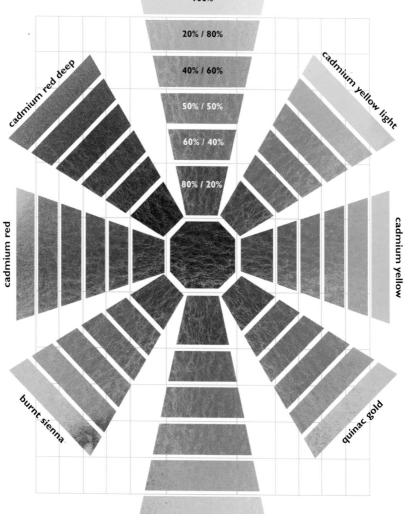

lemon yellow

100%

20% / 80%

40% / 60%

50% / 50%

60% / 40%

80% / 20%

cadmium red deep

cadmium yellow light

cadmium red

cadmium yellow

burnt sienna

quinac gold

raw sienna

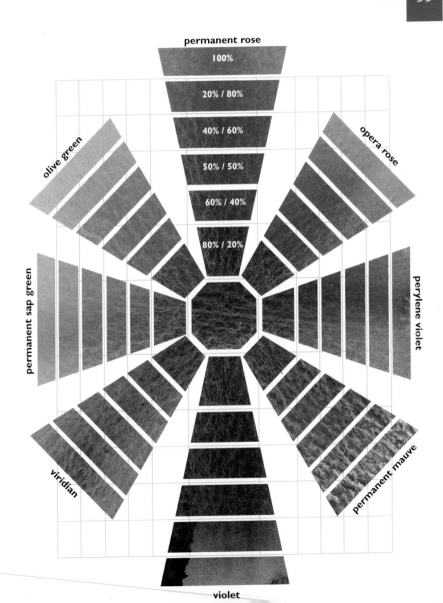

permanent rose

100%

20% / 80%

40% / 60%

50% / 50%

60% / 40%

80% / 20%

olive green

opera rose

permanent sap green

perylene violet

viridian

permanent mauve

violet

cobalt blue

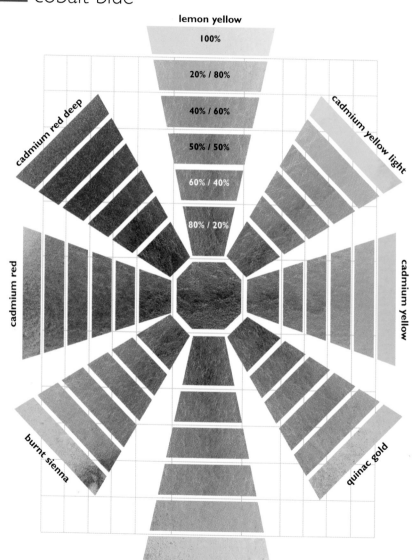

lemon yellow

100%

20% / 80%

40% / 60%

50% / 50%

60% / 40%

80% / 20%

cadmium red deep

cadmium yellow light

cadmium red

cadmium yellow

burnt sienna

quinac gold

raw sienna

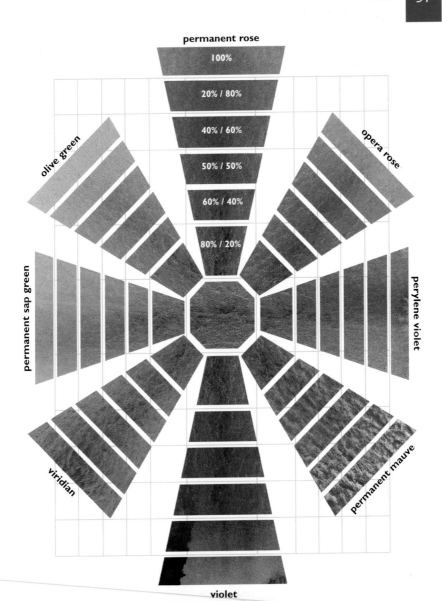

permanent rose

100%

20% / 80%

40% / 60%

50% / 50%

60% / 40%

80% / 20%

olive green

opera rose

permanent sap green

perylene violet

viridian

permanent mauve

violet

cerulean blue

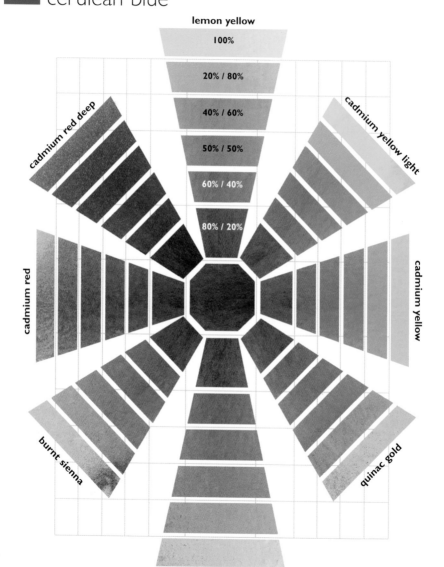

lemon yellow
100%
20% / 80%
40% / 60%
50% / 50%
60% / 40%
80% / 20%

cadmium red deep

cadmium yellow light

cadmium red

cadmium yellow

burnt sienna

quinac gold

raw sienna

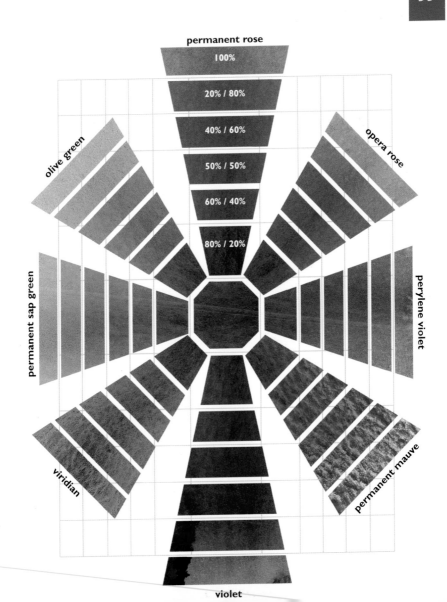

permanent rose

100%

20% / 80%

40% / 60%

50% / 50%

60% / 40%

80% / 20%

olive green

opera rose

permanent sap green

perylene violet

viridian

permanent mauve

violet

Prussian blue

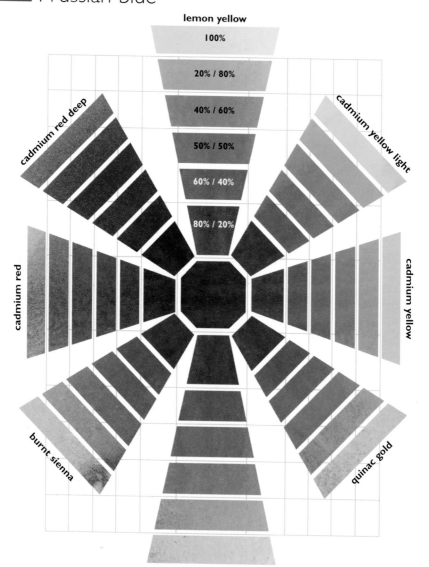

lemon yellow

100%

20% / 80%

40% / 60%

50% / 50%

60% / 40%

80% / 20%

cadmium red deep

cadmium yellow light

cadmium red

cadmium yellow

burnt sienna

quinac gold

raw sienna

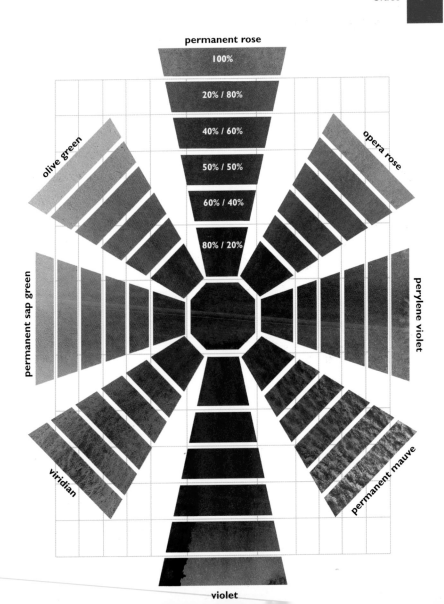

permanent rose

100%

20% / 80%

40% / 60%

50% / 50%

60% / 40%

80% / 20%

olive green

opera rose

permanent sap green

perylene violet

viridian

permanent mauve

violet

phthalo turquoise

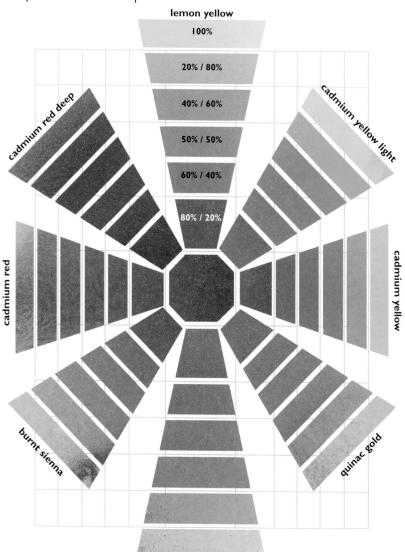

lemon yellow

100%

20% / 80%

40% / 60%

50% / 50%

60% / 40%

80% / 20%

cadmium red deep

cadmium yellow light

cadmium red

cadmium yellow

burnt sienna

quinac gold

raw sienna

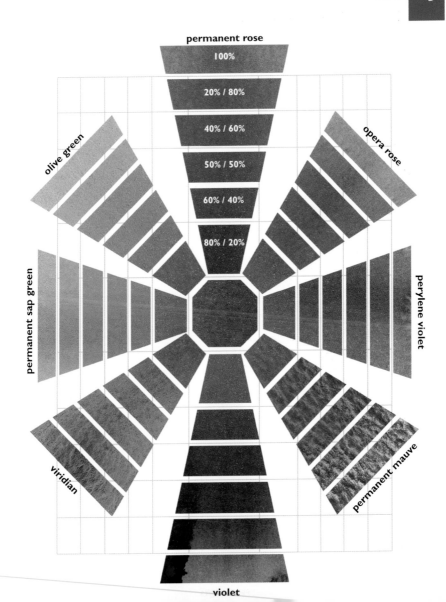

viridian

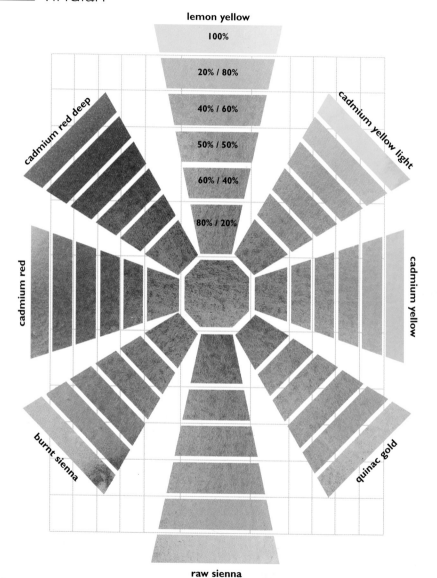

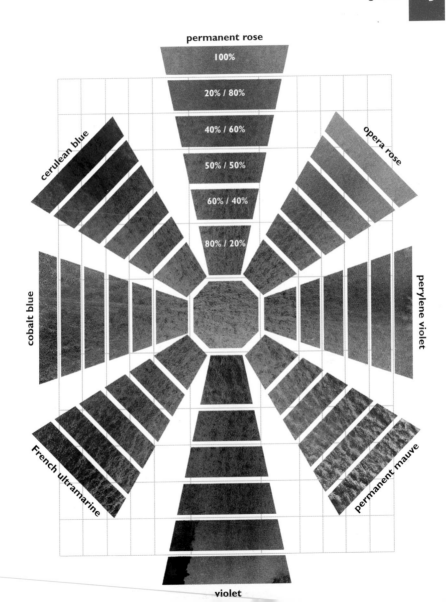

permanent rose

100%

20% / 80%

40% / 60%

50% / 50%

60% / 40%

80% / 20%

cerulean blue

opera rose

cobalt blue

perylene violet

French ultramarine

permanent mauve

violet

permanent sap green

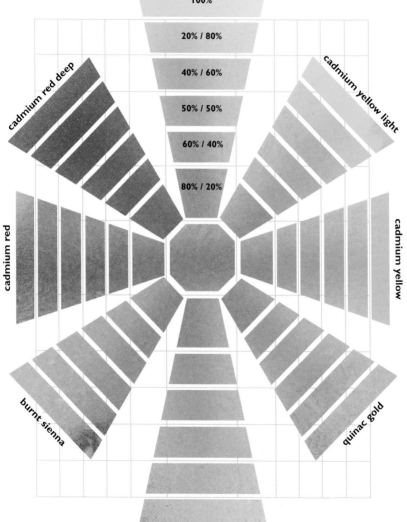

lemon yellow
100%

20% / 80%

40% / 60%

50% / 50%

60% / 40%

80% / 20%

cadmium red deep

cadmium yellow light

cadmium red

cadmium yellow

burnt sienna

quinac gold

raw sienna

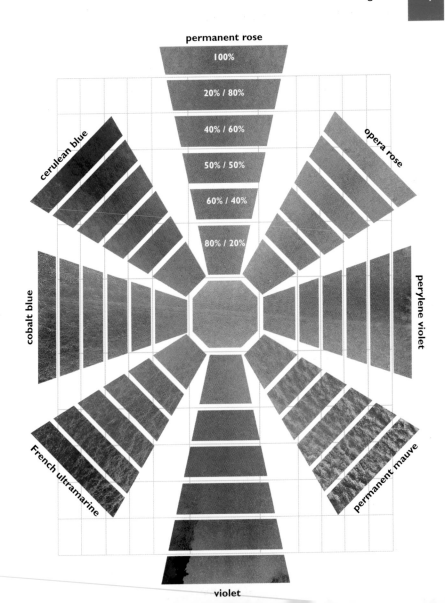

permanent rose

100%

20% / 80%

40% / 60%

50% / 50%

60% / 40%

80% / 20%

cerulean blue

opera rose

cobalt blue

perylene violet

French ultramarine

permanent mauve

violet

olive green

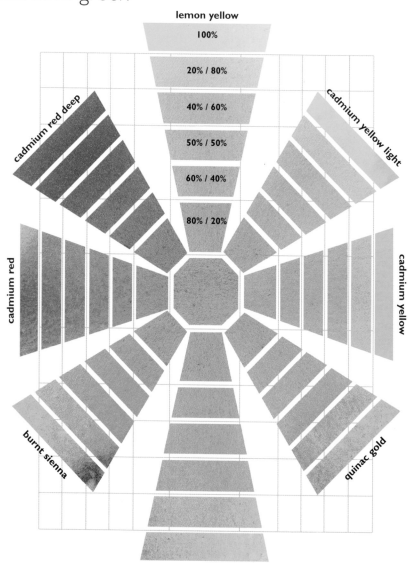

lemon yellow

100%

20% / 80%

40% / 60%

50% / 50%

60% / 40%

80% / 20%

cadmium red deep

cadmium yellow light

cadmium red

cadmium yellow

burnt sienna

quinac gold

raw sienna

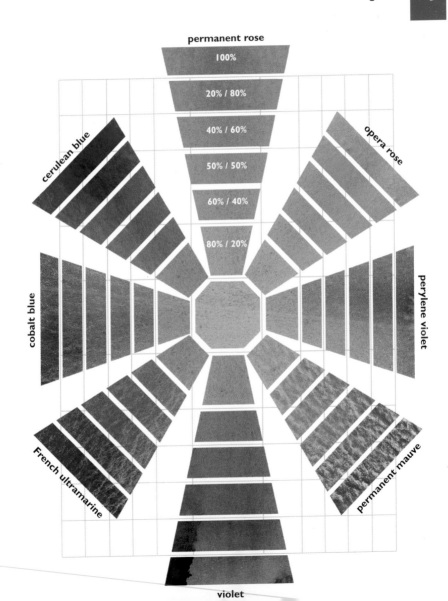

permanent rose

100%

20% / 80%

40% / 60%

50% / 50%

60% / 40%

80% / 20%

cerulean blue

opera rose

cobalt blue

perylene violet

French ultramarine

permanent mauve

violet

raw umber

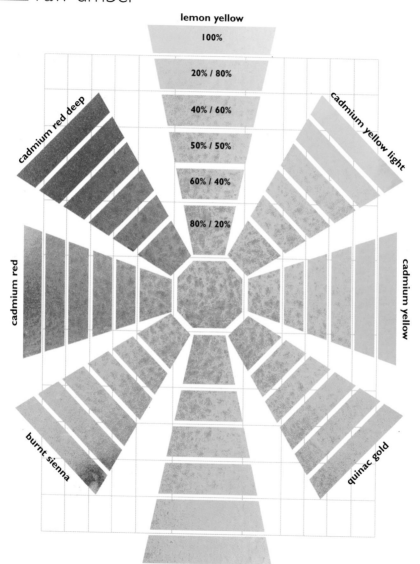

lemon yellow

100%

20% / 80%

40% / 60%

50% / 50%

60% / 40%

80% / 20%

cadmium red deep

cadmium yellow light

cadmium red

cadmium yellow

burnt sienna

quinac gold

raw sienna

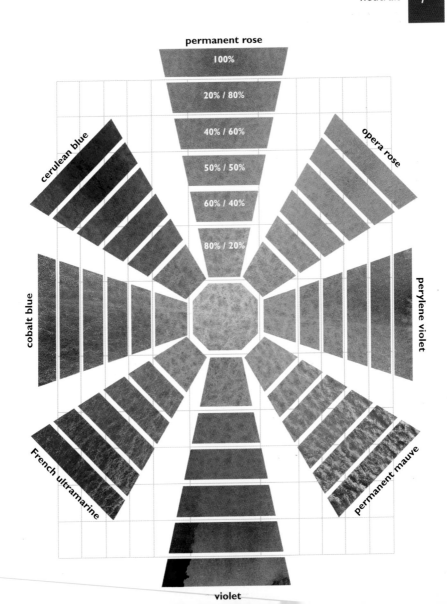

permanent rose

100%

20% / 80%

40% / 60%

50% / 50%

60% / 40%

80% / 20%

cerulean blue

opera rose

cobalt blue

perylene violet

French ultramarine

permanent mauve

violet

burnt umber

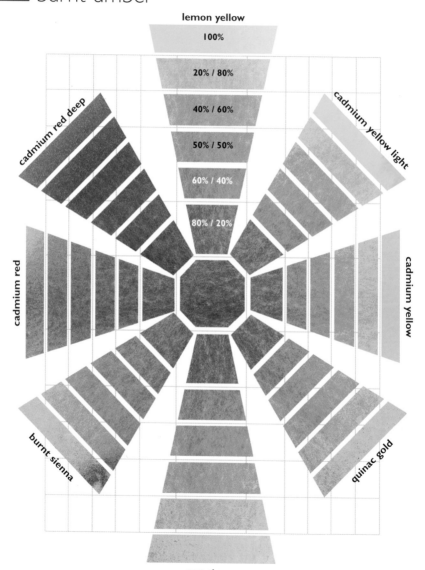

lemon yellow

100%

20% / 80%

40% / 60%

50% / 50%

60% / 40%

80% / 20%

cadmium red deep

cadmium yellow light

cadmium red

cadmium yellow

burnt sienna

quinac gold

raw sienna

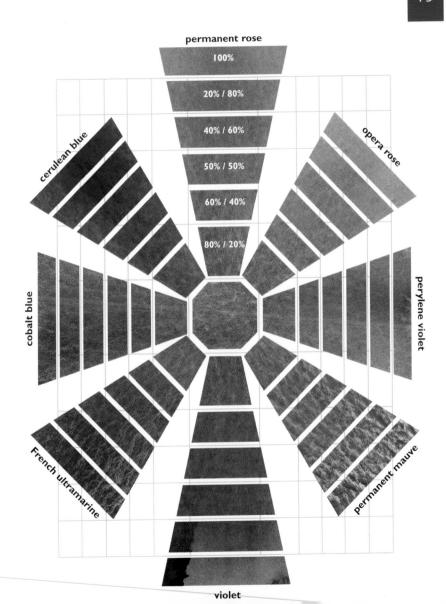

permanent rose

100%

20% / 80%

40% / 60%

50% / 50%

60% / 40%

80% / 20%

cerulean blue

opera rose

cobalt blue

perylene violet

French ultramarine

permanent mauve

violet

sepia

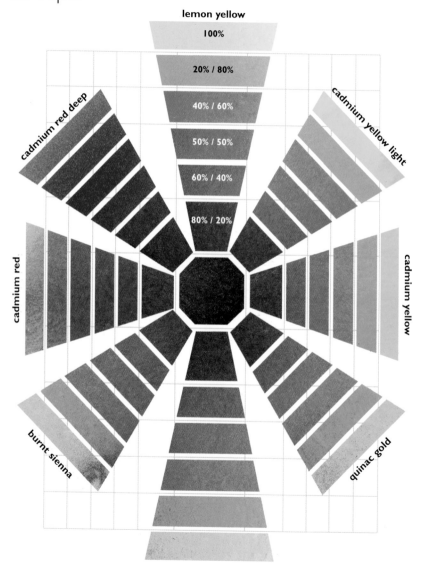

lemon yellow
100%
20% / 80%
40% / 60%
50% / 50%
60% / 40%
80% / 20%

cadmium red deep

cadmium yellow light

cadmium red

cadmium yellow

burnt sienna

quinac gold

raw sienna

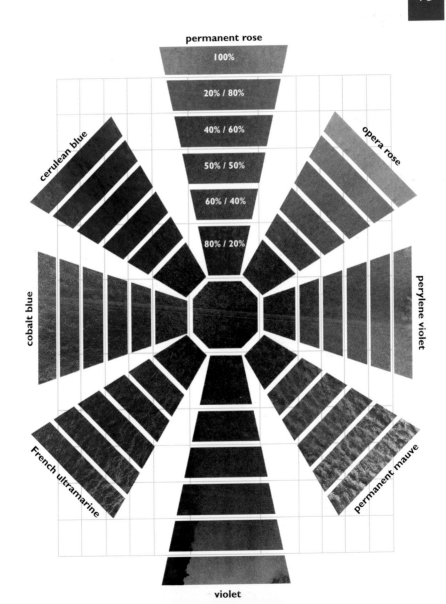

permanent rose

100%

20% / 80%

40% / 60%

50% / 50%

60% / 40%

80% / 20%

cerulean blue

opera rose

cobalt blue

perylene violet

French ultramarine

permanent mauve

violet

Payne's gray

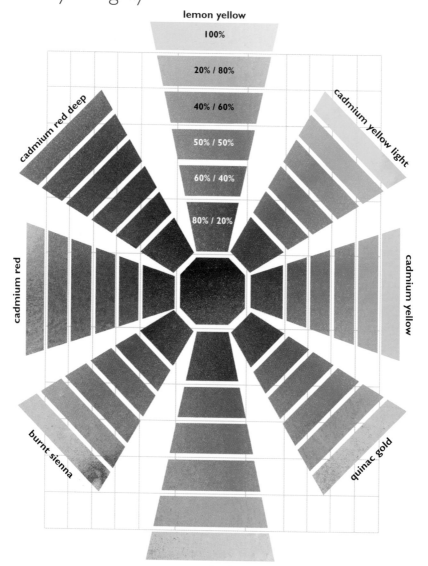

lemon yellow

100%

20% / 80%

40% / 60%

50% / 50%

60% / 40%

80% / 20%

cadmium red deep

cadmium yellow light

cadmium red

cadmium yellow

burnt sienna

quinac gold

raw sienna

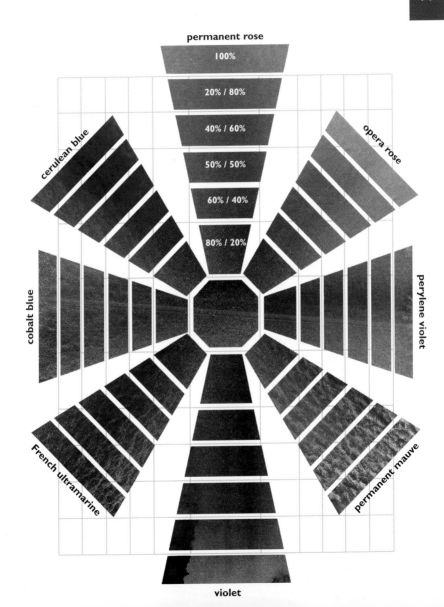

permanent rose

100%

20% / 80%

40% / 60%

50% / 50%

60% / 40%

80% / 20%

cerulean blue

opera rose

cobalt blue

perylene violet

French ultramarine

permanent mauve

violet

acrylic colour mixes

The following pages feature 25 of the most widely used acrylic colours by amateur and professional artists. The mixes provide excellent evidence that you do not need a huge collection of paints to produce a wide range of bright, vibrant colours, whatever your subject. Use these mixes as guides to help you achieve the exact shade you want.

supports and brushes

Painting in acrylics can be done on almost any surface. A surface that has been covered with a brilliant white will give the brightest effects when transparent washes are used. Transparent washes work well on many kinds of paper including those made for watercolour painting. When the paints are made opaque by the addition of white, the colour of the ground becomes less important.

Canvas, paper, card, hardboard, MDF (medium-density fibreboard), unglazed ceramics, even non-ferrous metal, as long as it has some texture to aid adhesion, can all give good results and make possible a vast range of effects. Acrylics are ideal for mural painting. The advent of acrylics has encouraged experimentation and made painting and craft work easier and more accessible to more people.

An easel is a useful addition to your acrylic painting kit. If you keep all your paints, papers, brushes, and other supports together between sessions, everything you need is readily at hand when you want to paint.

BRUSHES AND TOOLS

Any means of applying paint can be used with acrylics. Usable tools range from the fine sable brushes, used for professional illustration, to the knives and modeling tools used on textured abstract work, which have expressive possibilities when used with acrylics.

When selecting brushes choose at least one broad flat brush for laying washes, as well as several different-sized round brushes. Filberts, far right, allow you to produce soft, tapered marks, and are good for softening edges.

Traditional hogs hair brushes are excellent for acrylics, as are polyester and synthetic fibres. Rollers can be used in many types of picture making and a wire brush can even be used to leave furrows and stipple marks in wet paint.

A wide range of brushes made by many manufacturers are specially designed for use with acrylics, and their firm but flexible hairs work well with the traditional styles of painting.

A word of warning: Be scrupulous about washing your brushes immediately after use. Once the chemical drying process has begun, it cannot be reversed. Wash your brushes in clean water until the water runs clear, and ensure that there is no paint left between the hairs near the metal ferrule. Some soap or dishwashing liquid will help you keep your brushes clean and reusable.

Acrylic colours can be used on canvas and, once they are dry, give results comparable to oil colours.

the acrylics palette

These are the most popular acrylics manufactured, available in art stores and via the Internet. Colours included in many preselected paint boxes are also chosen from this range.

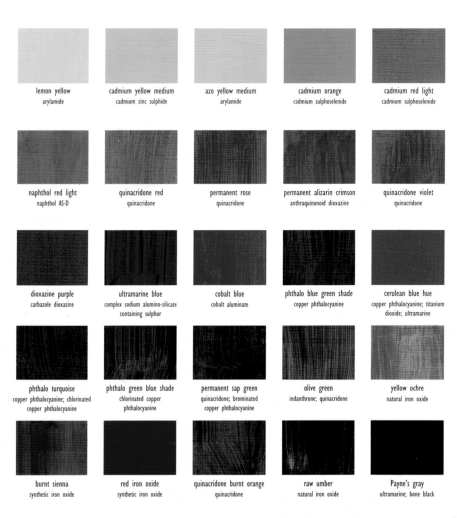

lemon yellow
arylamide

cadmium yellow medium
cadmium zinc sulphide

azo yellow medium
arylamide

cadmium orange
cadmium sulphoselenide

cadmium red light
cadmium sulphoselenide

naphthol red light
naphthol AS-D

quinacridone red
quinacridone

permanent rose
quinacridone

permanent alizarin crimson
anthraquinonoid dioxazine

quinacridone violet
quinacridone

dioxazine purple
carbazole dioxazine

ultramarine blue
complex sodium alumino-silicate
containing sulphur

cobalt blue
cobalt aluminate

phthalo blue green shade
copper phthalocyanine

cerulean blue hue
copper phthalocyanine; titanium
dioxide; ultramarine

phthalo turquoise
copper phthalocyanine; chlorinated
copper phthalocyanine

phthalo green blue shade
chlorinated copper
phthalocyanine

permanent sap green
quinacridone; brominated
copper phthalocyanine

olive green
indanthrone; quinacridone

yellow ochre
natural iron oxide

burnt sienna
synthetic iron oxide

red iron oxide
synthetic iron oxide

quinacridone burnt orange
quinacridone

raw umber
natural iron oxide

Payne's gray
ultramarine; bone black

SUGGESTED PALETTES

It is a good idea for beginners to start with a very restricted palette of six colours and use the charts referring to these six colours to develop their colour skills and discover their preferences. They can then augment their palette as they gain experience. A good minimum palette for a beginner is shown here:

lemon yellow

cadmium red light

ultramarine blue

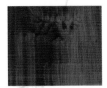

burnt sienna

phthalo green blue shade

dioxazine purple

Acrylic colours are available in a broad range of colours, and can be mixed together to create many more shades. Mix in a palette or on a plate to get the precise colour you want.

lemon yellow

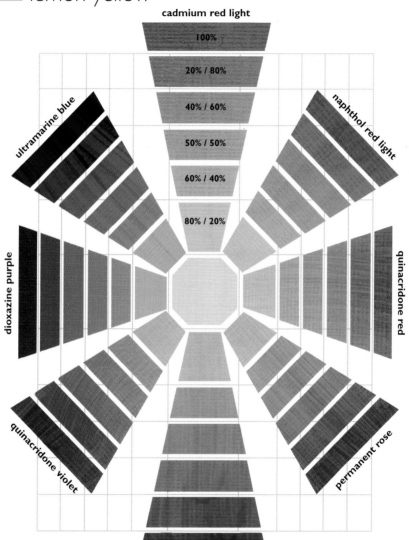

cadmium red light

100%

20% / 80%

40% / 60%

50% / 50%

60% / 40%

80% / 20%

ultramarine blue

naphthol red light

dioxazine purple

quinacridone red

quinacridone violet

permanent rose

permanent alizarin crimson

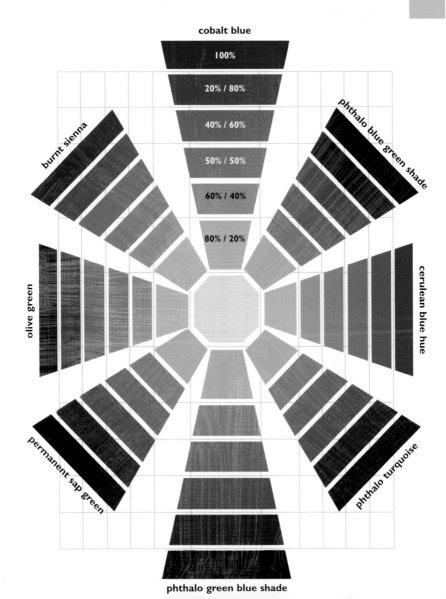

cobalt blue

100%

20% / 80%

40% / 60%

50% / 50%

60% / 40%

80% / 20%

burnt sienna

phthalo blue green shade

olive green

cerulean blue hue

permanent sap green

phthalo turquoise

phthalo green blue shade

cadmium yellow medium

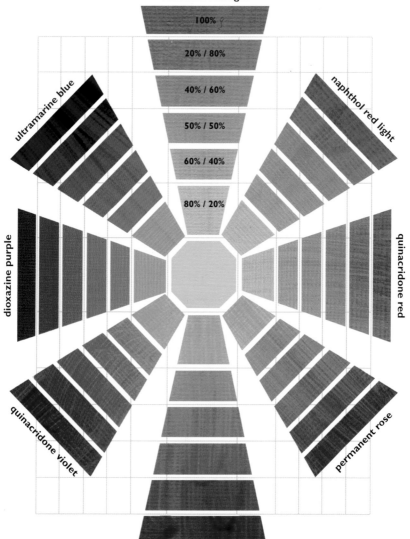

cadmium red light

100%

20% / 80%

40% / 60%

50% / 50%

60% / 40%

80% / 20%

ultramarine blue

naphthol red light

dioxazine purple

quinacridone red

quinacridone violet

permanent rose

permanent alizarin crimson

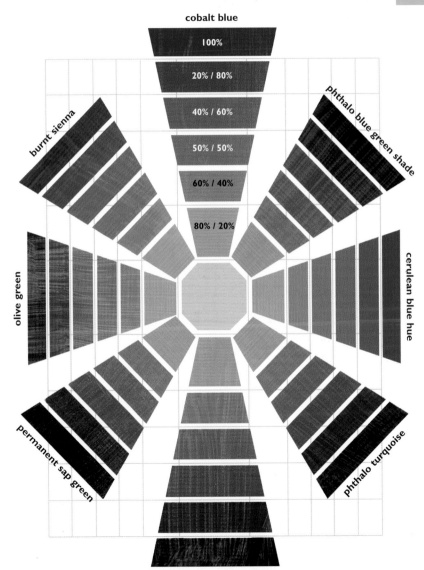

cobalt blue

100%

20% / 80%

40% / 60%

50% / 50%

60% / 40%

80% / 20%

phthalo blue green shade

burnt sienna

olive green

cerulean blue hue

permanent sap green

phthalo turquoise

phthalo green blue shade

azo yellow medium

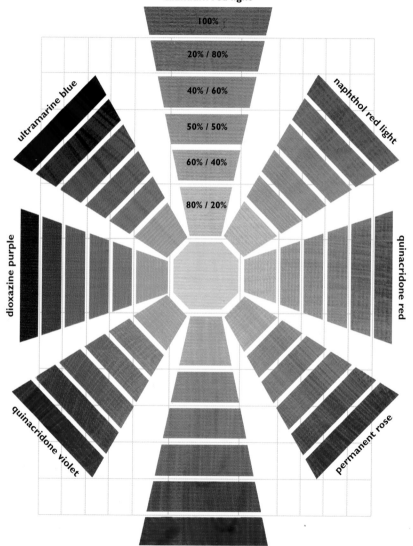

cadmium red light

100%

20% / 80%

40% / 60%

50% / 50%

60% / 40%

80% / 20%

ultramarine blue

naphthol red light

dioxazine purple

quinacridone red

quinacridone violet

permanent rose

permanent alizarin crimson

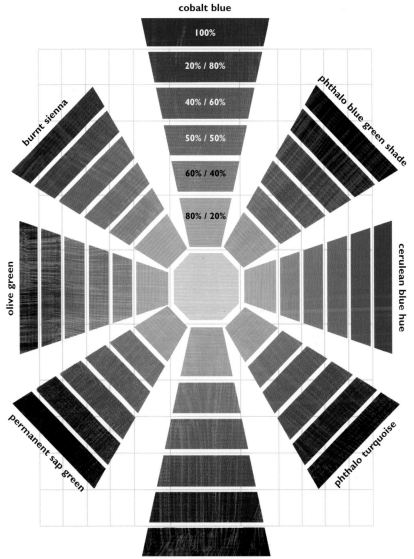

cobalt blue

100%

20% / 80%

40% / 60%

50% / 50%

60% / 40%

80% / 20%

burnt sienna

phthalo blue green shade

olive green

cerulean blue hue

permanent sap green

phthalo turquoise

phthalo green blue shade

cadmium orange

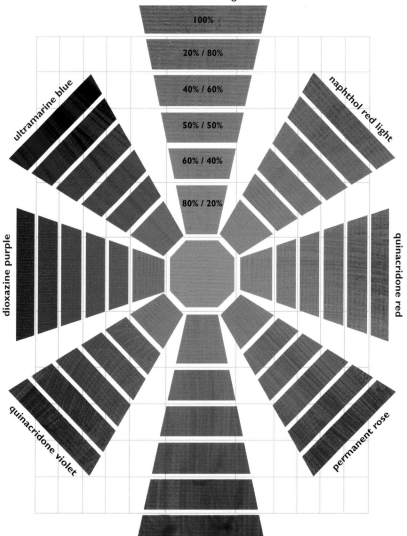

cadmium red light

100%

20% / 80%

40% / 60%

50% / 50%

60% / 40%

80% / 20%

ultramarine blue

naphthol red light

dioxazine purple

quinacridone red

quinacridone violet

permanent rose

permanent alizarin crimson

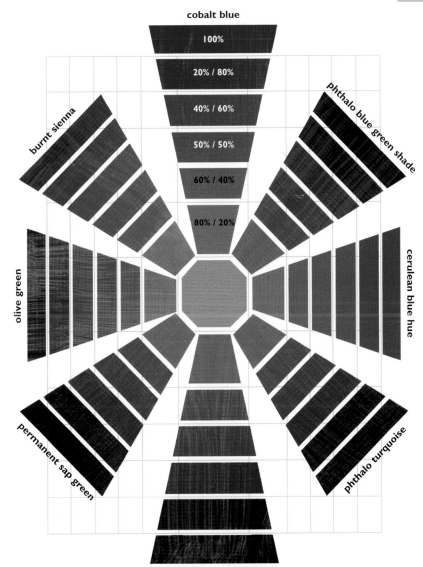

cobalt blue

100%

20% / 80%

40% / 60%

50% / 50%

60% / 40%

80% / 20%

burnt sienna

phthalo blue green shade

olive green

cerulean blue hue

permanent sap green

phthalo turquoise

phthalo green blue shade

cadmium red light

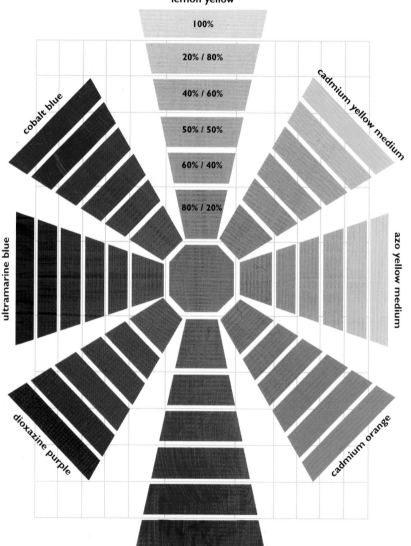

lemon yellow

100%

20% / 80%

40% / 60%

50% / 50%

60% / 40%

80% / 20%

cobalt blue

cadmium yellow medium

ultramarine blue

azo yellow medium

dioxazine purple

cadmium orange

quinacridone violet

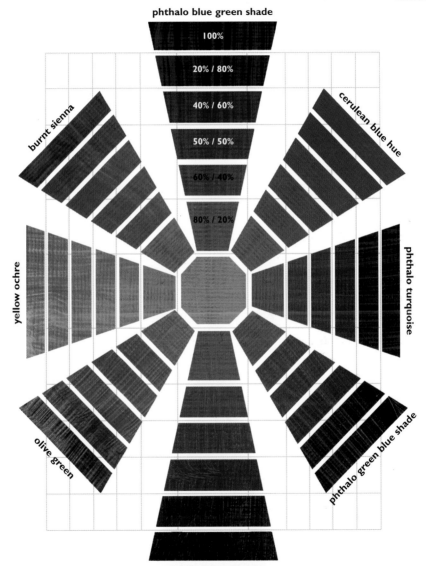

phthalo blue green shade

100%

20% / 80%

40% / 60%

50% / 50%

60% / 40%

80% / 20%

burnt sienna

cerulean blue hue

yellow ochre

phthalo turquoise

olive green

phthalo green blue shade

permanent sap green

naphthol red light

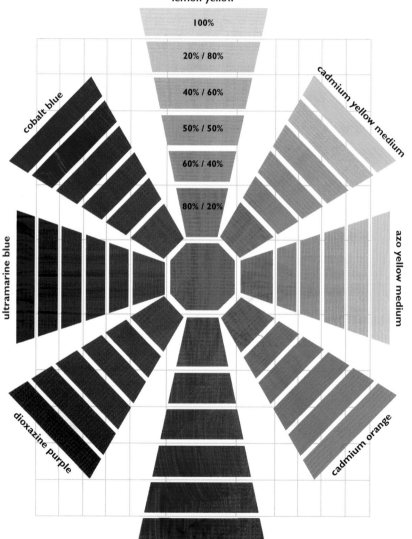

lemon yellow

100%

20% / 80%

40% / 60%

50% / 50%

60% / 40%

80% / 20%

cobalt blue

cadmium yellow medium

ultramarine blue

azo yellow medium

dioxazine purple

cadmium orange

quinacridone violet

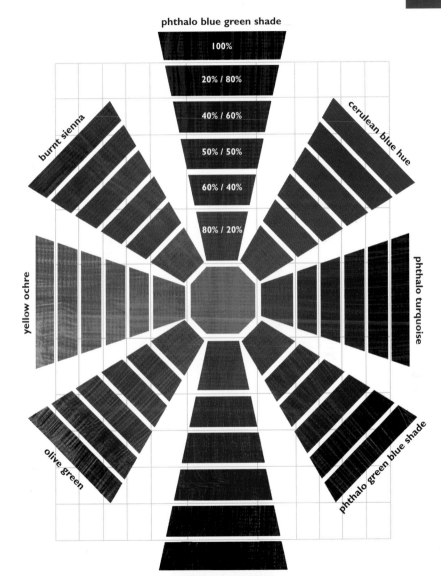

phthalo blue green shade

100%

20% / 80%

40% / 60%

50% / 50%

60% / 40%

80% / 20%

burnt sienna

cerulean blue hue

yellow ochre

phthalo turquoise

olive green

phthalo green blue shade

permanent sap green

quinacridone red

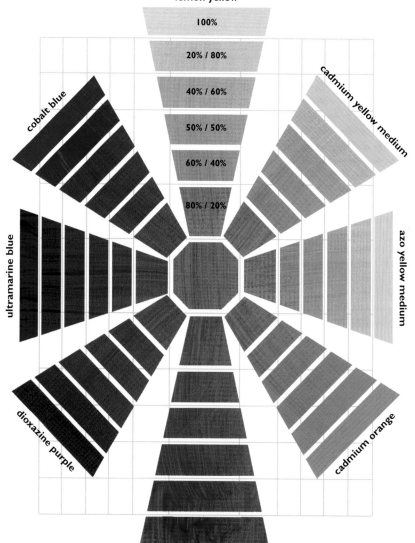

lemon yellow

100%

20% / 80%

40% / 60%

50% / 50%

60% / 40%

80% / 20%

cadmium yellow medium

cobalt blue

azo yellow medium

ultramarine blue

cadmium orange

dioxazine purple

quinacridone violet

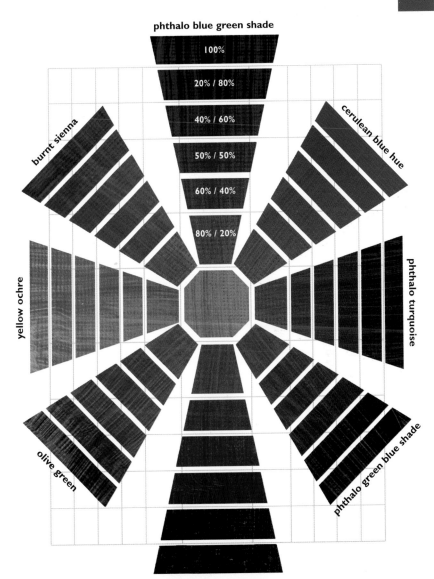

phthalo blue green shade

100%

20% / 80%

40% / 60%

50% / 50%

60% / 40%

80% / 20%

burnt sienna

cerulean blue hue

yellow ochre

phthalo turquoise

olive green

phthalo green blue shade

permanent sap green

permanent rose

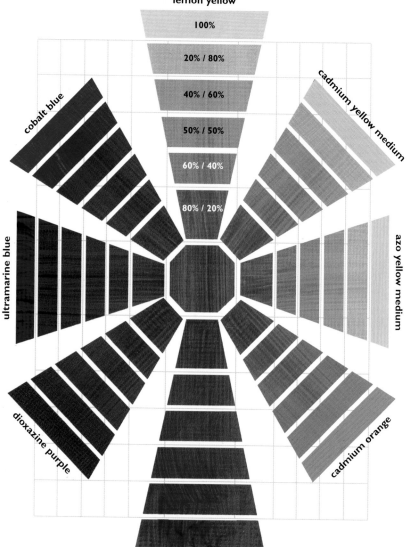

lemon yellow

100%

20% / 80%

40% / 60%

50% / 50%

60% / 40%

80% / 20%

cobalt blue

cadmium yellow medium

ultramarine blue

azo yellow medium

dioxazine purple

cadmium orange

quinacridone violet

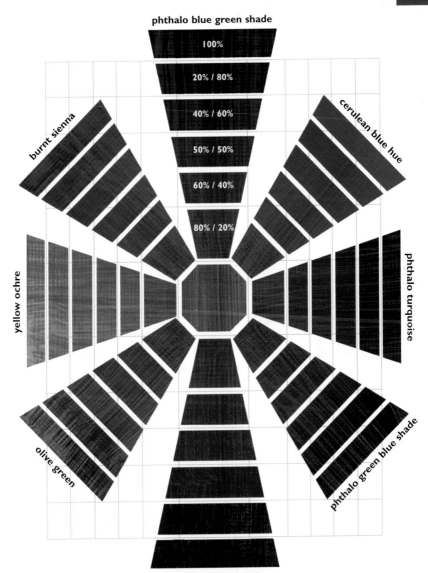

phthalo blue green shade

100%

20% / 80%

40% / 60%

50% / 50%

60% / 40%

80% / 20%

burnt sienna

cerulean blue hue

yellow ochre

phthalo turquoise

olive green

phthalo green blue shade

permanent sap green

permanent alizarin crimson

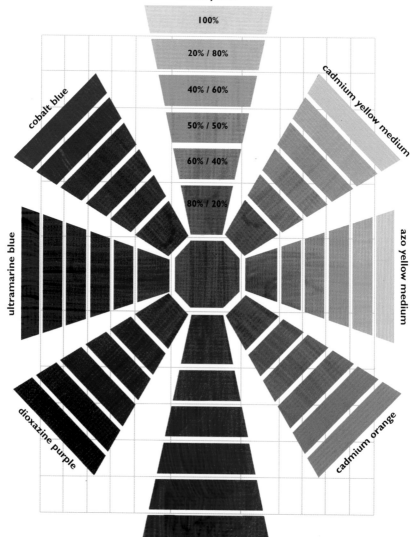

lemon yellow

100%

20% / 80%

40% / 60%

50% / 50%

60% / 40%

80% / 20%

cobalt blue

cadmium yellow medium

ultramarine blue

azo yellow medium

dioxazine purple

cadmium orange

quinacridone violet

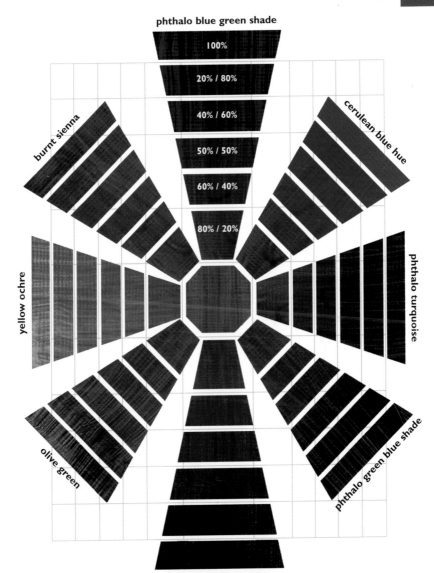

phthalo blue green shade

100%

20% / 80%

40% / 60%

50% / 50%

60% / 40%

80% / 20%

burnt sienna

cerulean blue hue

yellow ochre

phthalo turquoise

olive green

phthalo green blue shade

permanent sap green

quinacridone violet

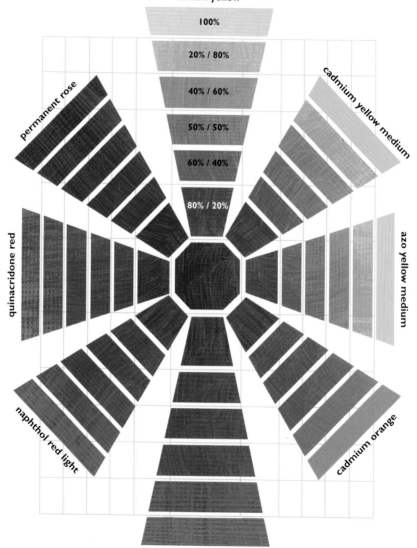

lemon yellow

100%

20% / 80%

40% / 60%

50% / 50%

60% / 40%

80% / 20%

permanent rose

cadmium yellow medium

quinacridone red

azo yellow medium

naphthol red light

cadmium orange

cadmium red light

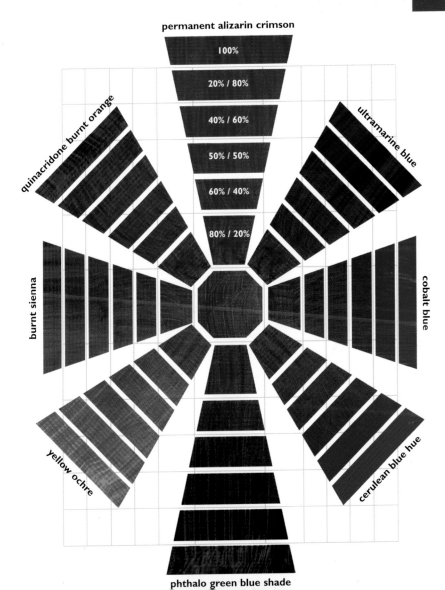

permanent alizarin crimson

100%

20% / 80%

40% / 60%

50% / 50%

60% / 40%

80% / 20%

quinacridone burnt orange

ultramarine blue

burnt sienna

cobalt blue

yellow ochre

cerulean blue hue

phthalo green blue shade

dioxazine purple

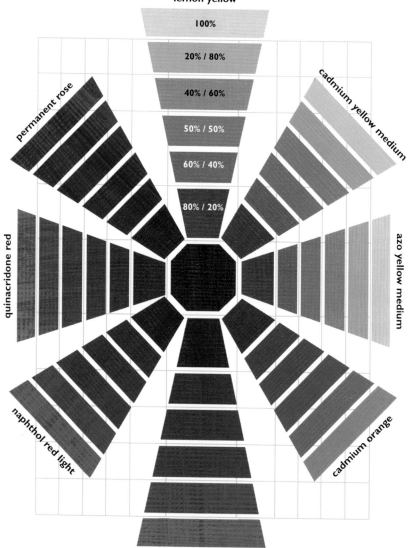

lemon yellow

100%

20% / 80%

40% / 60%

50% / 50%

60% / 40%

80% / 20%

permanent rose

cadmium yellow medium

quinacridone red

azo yellow medium

naphthol red light

cadmium orange

cadmium red light

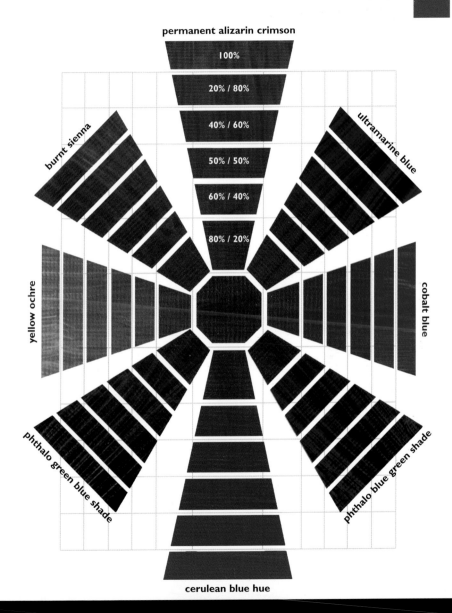

permanent alizarin crimson

100%

20% / 80%

40% / 60%

50% / 50%

60% / 40%

80% / 20%

burnt sienna

ultramarine blue

yellow ochre

cobalt blue

phthalo green blue shade

phthalo blue green shade

cerulean blue hue

more blue ▶▶ ▶▶ ▶▶

ultramarine blue

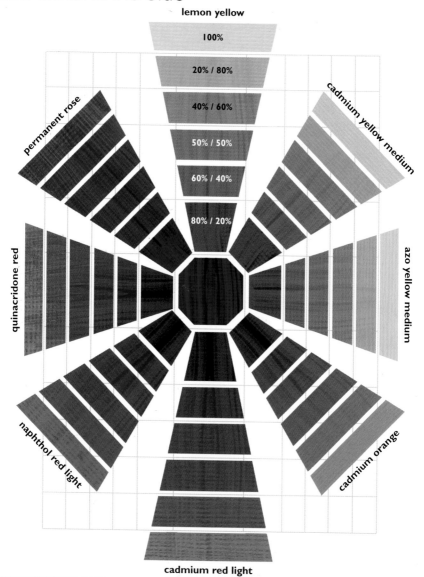

lemon yellow

100%

20% / 80%

40% / 60%

50% / 50%

60% / 40%

80% / 20%

permanent rose

cadmium yellow medium

quinacridone red

azo yellow medium

naphthol red light

cadmium orange

cadmium red light

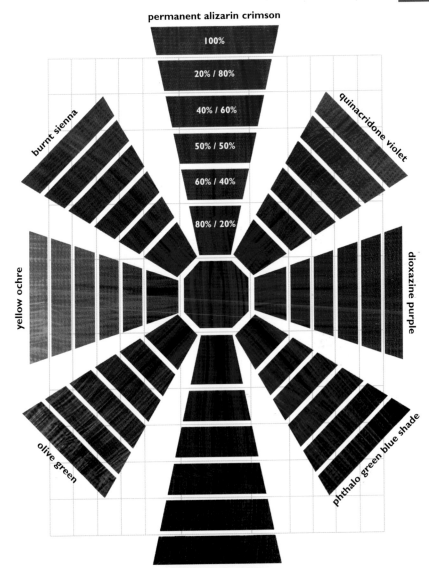

permanent alizarin crimson

100%

20% / 80%

40% / 60%

50% / 50%

60% / 40%

80% / 20%

burnt sienna

quinacridone violet

yellow ochre

dioxazine purple

olive green

phthalo green blue shade

permanent sap green

cobalt blue

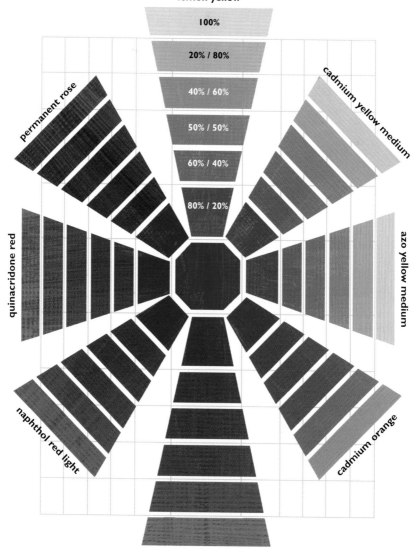

lemon yellow

100%

20% / 80%

40% / 60%

50% / 50%

60% / 40%

80% / 20%

permanent rose

cadmium yellow medium

quinacridone red

azo yellow medium

naphthol red light

cadmium orange

cadmium red light

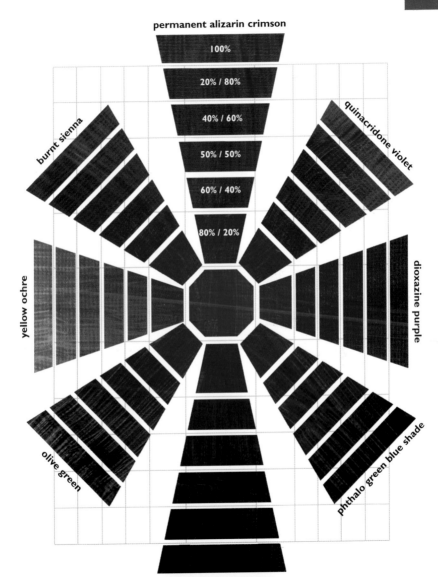

permanent alizarin crimson

100%

20% / 80%

40% / 60%

50% / 50%

60% / 40%

80% / 20%

burnt sienna

quinacridone violet

yellow ochre

dioxazine purple

olive green

phthalo green blue shade

permanent sap green

phthalo blue green shade

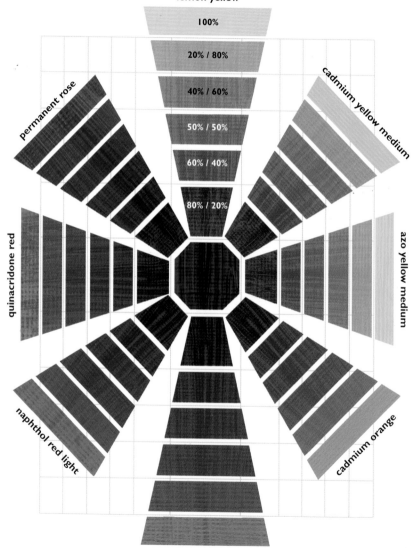

lemon yellow

100%

20% / 80%

40% / 60%

50% / 50%

60% / 40%

80% / 20%

permanent rose

cadmium yellow medium

quinacridone red

azo yellow medium

naphthol red light

cadmium orange

cadmium red light

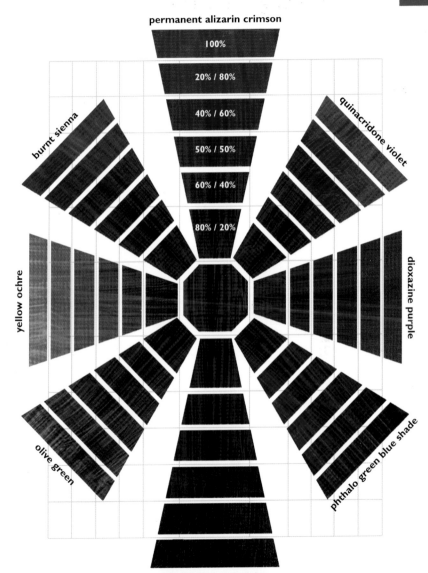

permanent alizarin crimson

100%

20% / 80%

40% / 60%

50% / 50%

60% / 40%

80% / 20%

burnt sienna

quinacridone violet

yellow ochre

dioxazine purple

olive green

phthalo green blue shade

permanent sap green

cerulean blue hue

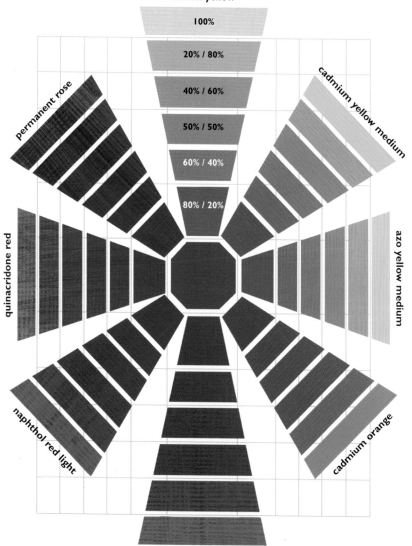

lemon yellow

100%

20% / 80%

40% / 60%

50% / 50%

60% / 40%

80% / 20%

permanent rose

cadmium yellow medium

quinacridone red

azo yellow medium

naphthol red light

cadmium orange

cadmium red light

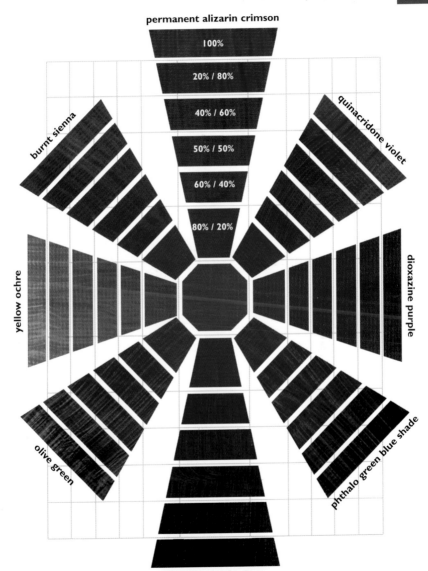

permanent alizarin crimson

100%

20% / 80%

40% / 60%

50% / 50%

60% / 40%

80% / 20%

burnt sienna

quinacridone violet

yellow ochre

dioxazine purple

olive green

phthalo green blue shade

permanent sap green

phthalo turquoise

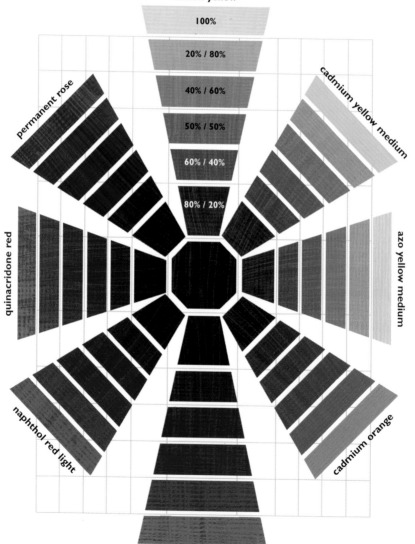

lemon yellow

100%

20% / 80%

40% / 60%

50% / 50%

60% / 40%

80% / 20%

cadmium yellow medium

permanent rose

azo yellow medium

quinacridone red

naphthol red light

cadmium orange

cadmium red light

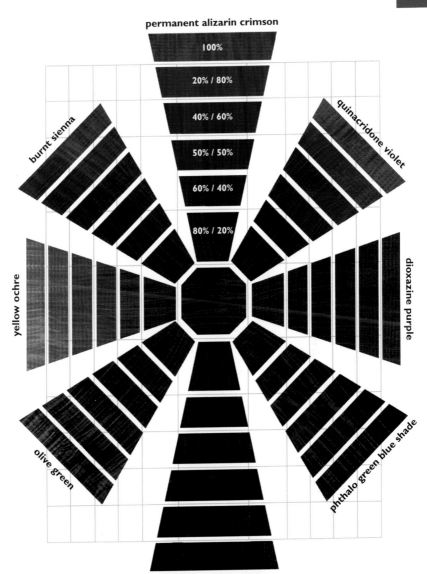

permanent alizarin crimson

100%

20% / 80%

40% / 60%

50% / 50%

60% / 40%

80% / 20%

burnt sienna

quinacridone violet

yellow ochre

dioxazine purple

olive green

phthalo green blue shade

permanent sap green

phthalo green blue shade

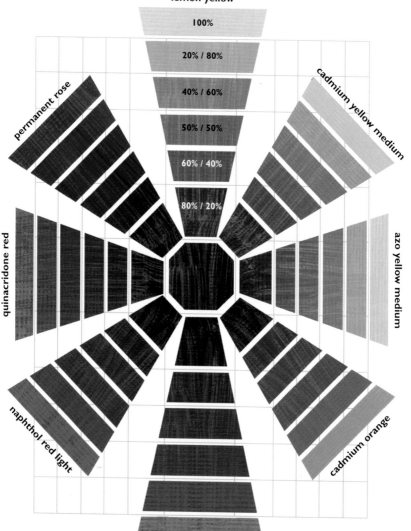

lemon yellow

100%

20% / 80%

40% / 60%

50% / 50%

60% / 40%

80% / 20%

cadmium yellow medium

permanent rose

azo yellow medium

quinacridone red

naphthol red light

cadmium orange

cadmium red light

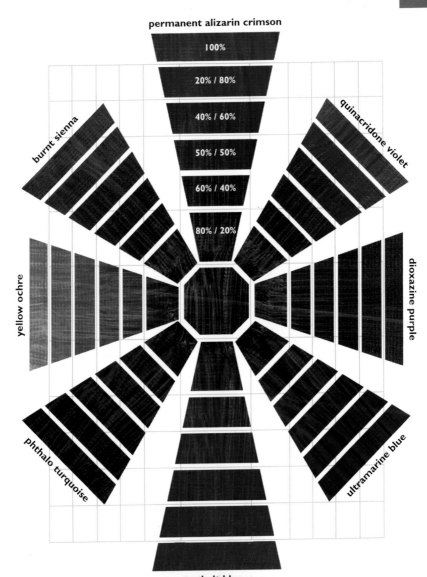

permanent alizarin crimson

100%

20% / 80%

40% / 60%

50% / 50%

60% / 40%

80% / 20%

burnt sienna

quinacridone violet

yellow ochre

dioxazine purple

phthalo turquoise

ultramarine blue

cobalt blue

permanent sap green

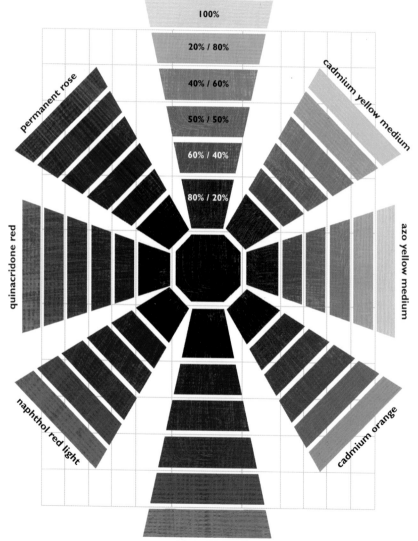

lemon yellow

100%

20% / 80%

40% / 60%

50% / 50%

60% / 40%

80% / 20%

permanent rose

cadmium yellow medium

quinacridone red

azo yellow medium

naphthol red light

cadmium orange

cadmium red light

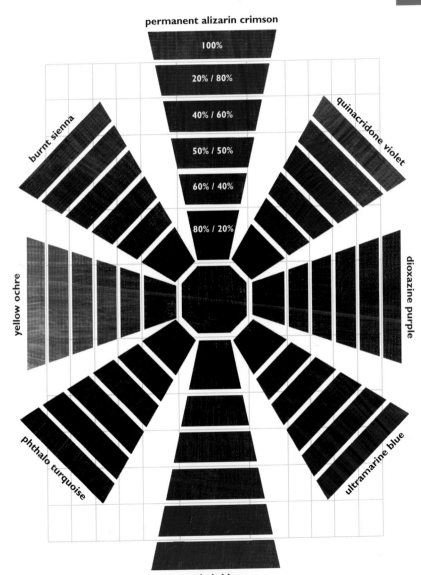

permanent alizarin crimson

100%

20% / 80%

40% / 60%

50% / 50%

60% / 40%

80% / 20%

burnt sienna

quinacridone violet

yellow ochre

dioxazine purple

phthalo turquoise

ultramarine blue

cobalt blue

olive green

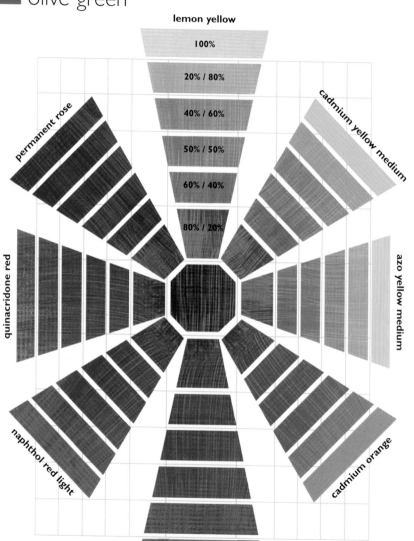

lemon yellow

100%

20% / 80%

40% / 60%

50% / 50%

60% / 40%

80% / 20%

permanent rose

cadmium yellow medium

quinacridone red

azo yellow medium

naphthol red light

cadmium orange

cadmium red light

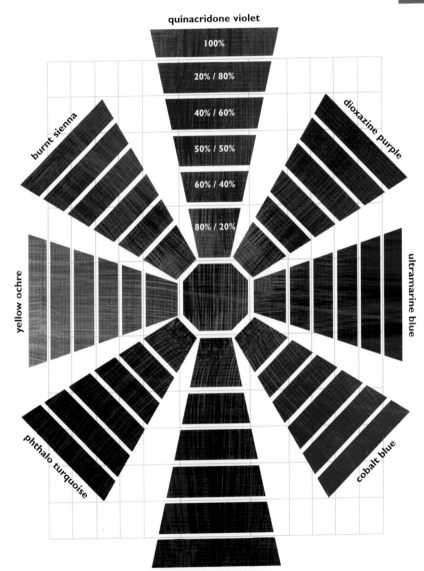

quinacridone violet

100%

20% / 80%

40% / 60%

50% / 50%

60% / 40%

80% / 20%

burnt sienna

dioxazine purple

yellow ochre

ultramarine blue

phthalo turquoise

cobalt blue

phthalo blue green shade

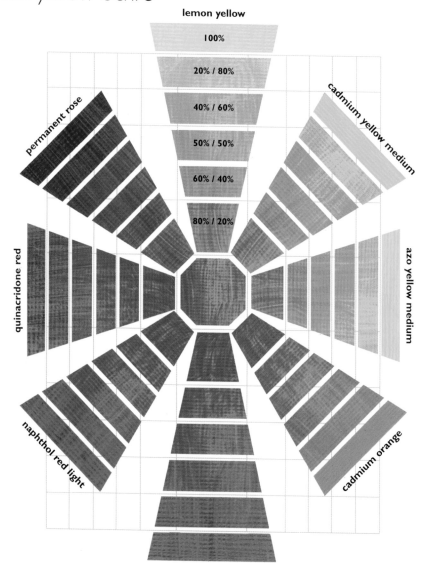

lemon yellow

100%

20% / 80%

40% / 60%

50% / 50%

60% / 40%

80% / 20%

permanent rose

cadmium yellow medium

quinacridone red

azo yellow medium

naphthol red light

cadmium orange

cadmium red light

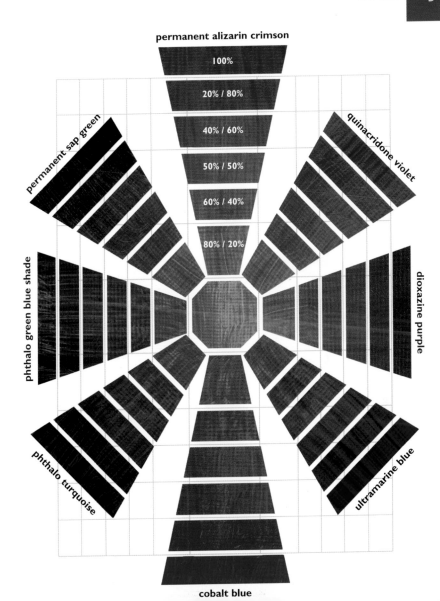

permanent alizarin crimson

100%

20% / 80%

40% / 60%

50% / 50%

60% / 40%

80% / 20%

permanent sap green

quinacridone violet

phthalo green blue shade

dioxazine purple

phthalo turquoise

ultramarine blue

cobalt blue

burnt sienna

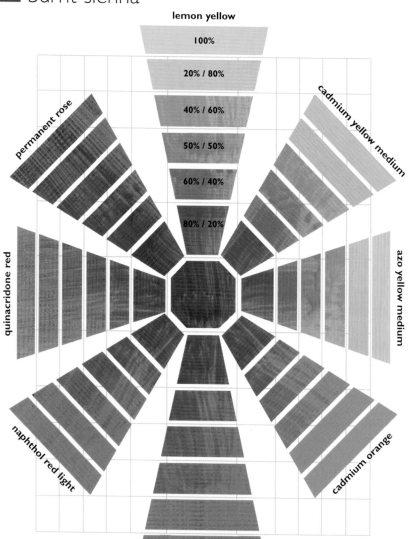

lemon yellow

100%

20% / 80%

40% / 60%

50% / 50%

60% / 40%

80% / 20%

permanent rose

cadmium yellow medium

quinacridone red

azo yellow medium

naphthol red light

cadmium orange

cadmium red light

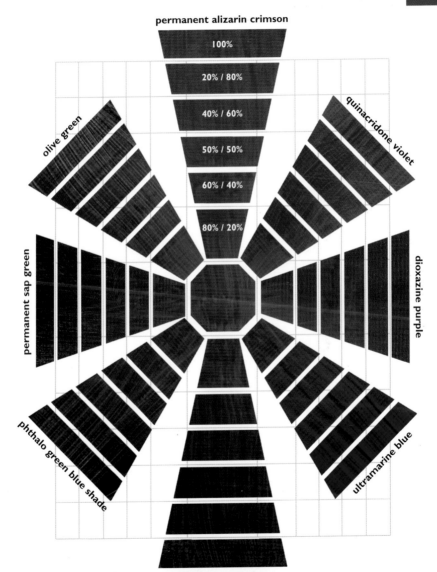

permanent alizarin crimson

100%

20% / 80%

40% / 60%

50% / 50%

60% / 40%

80% / 20%

olive green

quinacridone violet

permanent sap green

dioxazine purple

phthalo green blue shade

ultramarine blue

phthalo turquoise

red iron oxide

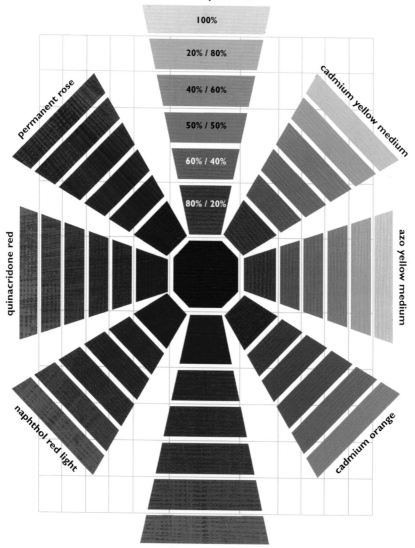

lemon yellow

100%

20% / 80%

40% / 60%

50% / 50%

60% / 40%

80% / 20%

permanent rose

cadmium yellow medium

quinacridone red

azo yellow medium

naphthol red light

cadmium orange

cadmium red light

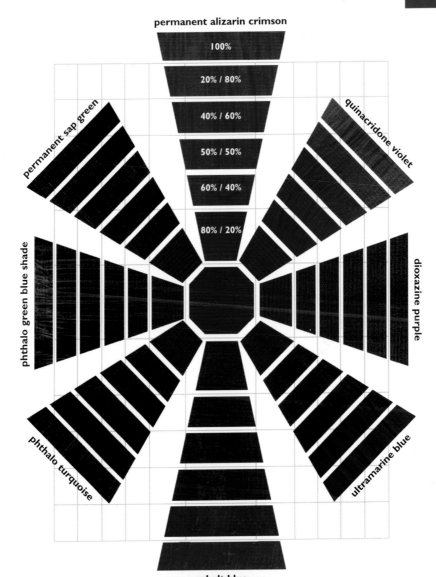

permanent alizarin crimson

100%

20% / 80%

40% / 60%

50% / 50%

60% / 40%

80% / 20%

permanent sap green

quinacridone violet

phthalo green blue shade

dioxazine purple

phthalo turquoise

ultramarine blue

cobalt blue

quinacridone burnt orange

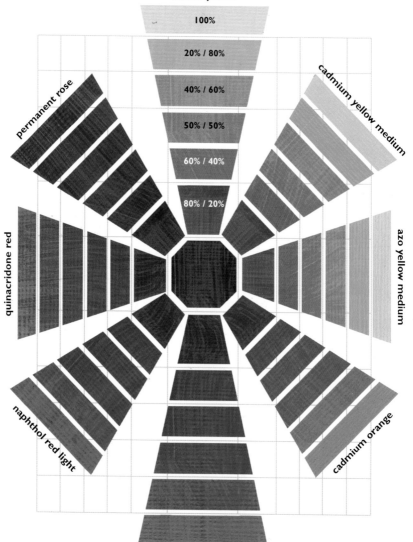

lemon yellow

100%

20% / 80%

40% / 60%

50% / 50%

60% / 40%

80% / 20%

permanent rose

cadmium yellow medium

quinacridone red

azo yellow medium

naphthol red light

cadmium orange

cadmium red light

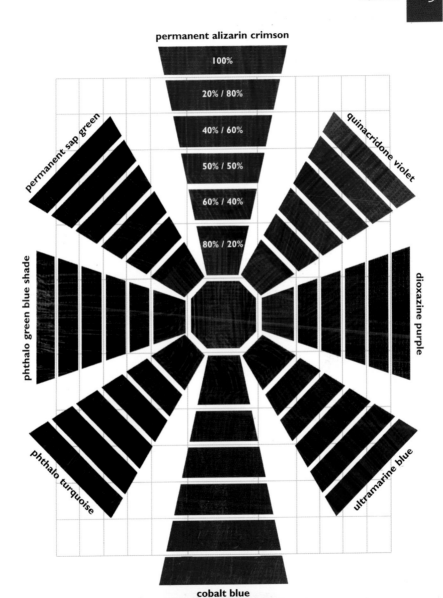

permanent alizarin crimson

100%

20% / 80%

40% / 60%

50% / 50%

60% / 40%

80% / 20%

quinacridone violet

permanent sap green

dioxazine purple

phthalo green blue shade

ultramarine blue

phthalo turquoise

cobalt blue

raw umber

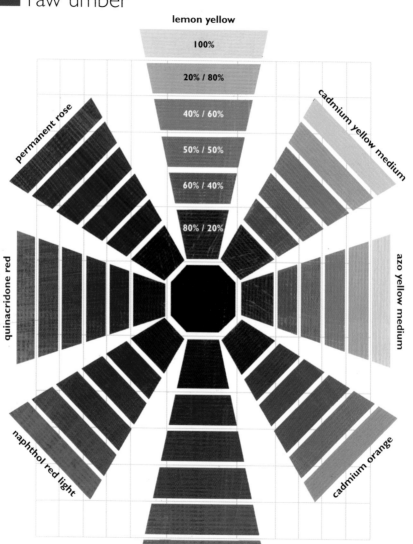

lemon yellow

100%

20% / 80%

40% / 60%

50% / 50%

60% / 40%

80% / 20%

cadmium yellow medium

permanent rose

azo yellow medium

quinacridone red

naphthol red light

cadmium orange

cadmium red light

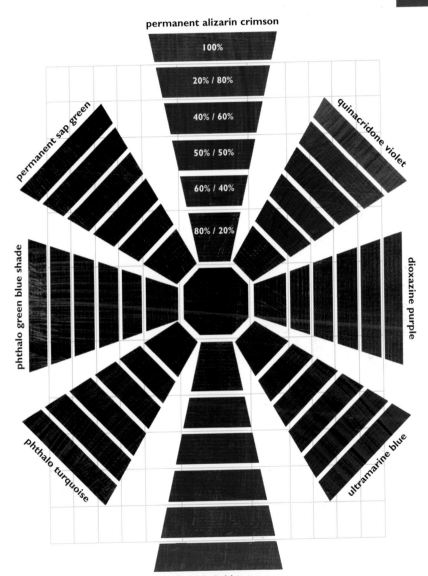

permanent alizarin crimson

100%

20% / 80%

40% / 60%

50% / 50%

60% / 40%

80% / 20%

permanent sap green

quinacridone violet

phthalo green blue shade

dioxazine purple

phthalo turquoise

ultramarine blue

cobalt blue

Payne's gray

lemon yellow

100%

20% / 80%

40% / 60%

50% / 50%

60% / 40%

80% / 20%

permanent rose

cadmium yellow medium

quinacridone red

azo yellow medium

naphthol red light

cadmium orange

cadmium red light

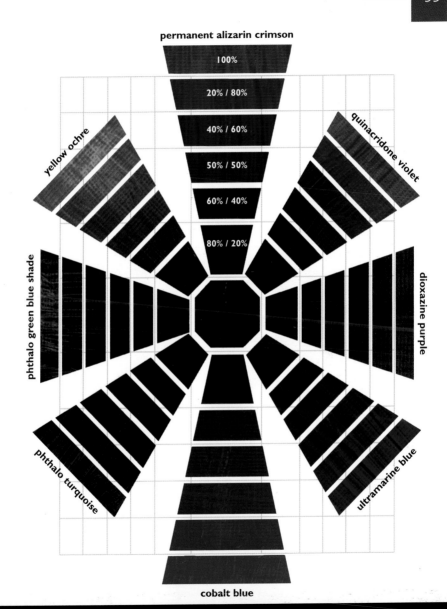

permanent alizarin crimson

100%

20% / 80%

40% / 60%

50% / 50%

60% / 40%

80% / 20%

yellow ochre

quinacridone violet

phthalo green blue shade

dioxazine purple

phthalo turquoise

ultramarine blue

cobalt blue

oil colour mixes

The following pages feature 25 main oil colours that are the most popular with amateur and professional artists. The mixes demonstrate that artists need very few colours to create an enormous range of bright, vibrant colours in oil paint. Use these mixes as guides to help you achieve the exact shade you want, whatever your subject.

supports and brushes

For mixing oil colours you need a flat, smooth surface that will not absorb the oil. The traditional palette in wood or plastic, including a thumb hole, is necessary for portrait and outdoor work, but in the studio many artists use a piece of glass, plastic, or glazed ceramic appropriate to the size of their paintings. The ultimate in economy is to use a glossy magazine and tear off each page when it is full.

Squeeze out each colour onto your palette as a long line of paint rather than as a large round blob. You will then be able to take colour from the end of the line without staining the rest of the paint: Any paint left will be clean for further use. Place each colour along the far edge of your palette so that you can see all the colours clearly. The order of the colours on the palette is a matter of personal choice, but do not change it too often, as this will slow down the work. One idea is to start with cool colours, the blues and violets, on the left, moving through the yellows to the ochres and earth colours with reds on the right. Place white and black on the extreme right.

A traditional paint box containing 12 or 24 tubes of colour, together with palette, brushes, and thinning oils, ensures everything is at hand when you are ready to paint.

SUPPORTS FOR OIL PAINTING

Wood panels, canvas, card-backed canvas, hardboard, MDF (medium-density fibreboard), card, and paper (properly primed to prevent the paint from sinking) are all suitable grounds for oil painting.

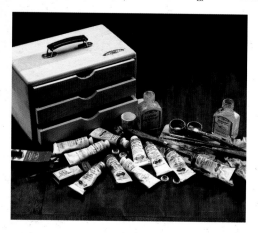

The difficulty and expense of joining wood to make large panels and their tendency to crack led to the use of canvas and other textiles that were lighter in weight and allowed much larger pictures to be made and hung. Pictures in the 19th century French Salons were sometimes 33 feet (10m) long. The woven texture of canvas allows every variation from smooth grain to extremely coarse to be used and gives the opportunity to elaborate yet more ways of painting with oils in the future.

BRUSHES

Hogs hair brushes are the most popular brushes for oil painting; they are the most effective when handling paint from tubes diluted, if at all, with a little turpentine. Paint dissolved with other liquids or resins requires softer fibres or hairs to enable you to obtain softer blending. Of these sable is still the best, but by a narrower margin than in the past. The various synthetic fibres offer good quality at a fraction of the cost of sable.

When you begin to use the opaque method of painting by adding white to alter the tone of the colours, use a palette knife to do the mixing so that your clean brush is ready to pick up just the amount of paint needed.

Many painters who favour a broader approach use palette knives and other painting tools either to add dramatic touches or to paint the whole picture.

Choose several hogs hair brushes in different sizes and shapes for your oil painting. This allows you to create works of art, whatever your style. Palette knives are useful additions.

the oil colour palette

These are the most popular oil colours with professional and amateur artists, available in art stores and via the Internet. Colours that are included in many pre-selected paint boxes are also chosen from this range.

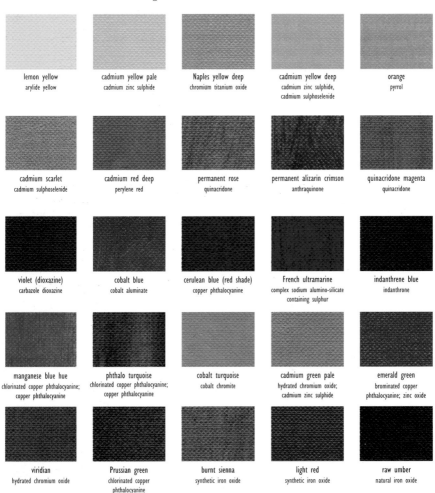

lemon yellow
arylide yellow

cadmium yellow pale
cadmium zinc sulphide

Naples yellow deep
chromium titanium oxide

cadmium yellow deep
cadmium zinc sulphide,
cadmium sulphoselenide

orange
pyrrol

cadmium scarlet
cadmium sulphoselenide

cadmium red deep
perylene red

permanent rose
quinacridone

permanent alizarin crimson
anthraquinone

quinacridone magenta
quinacridone

violet (dioxazine)
carbazole dioxazine

cobalt blue
cobalt aluminate

cerulean blue (red shade)
copper phthalocyanine

French ultramarine
complex sodium alumino-silicate
containing sulphur

indanthrene blue
indanthrone

manganese blue hue
chlorinated copper phthalocyanine;
copper phthalocyanine

phthalo turquoise
chlorinated copper phthalocyanine;
copper phthalocyanine

cobalt turquoise
cobalt chromite

cadmium green pale
hydrated chromium oxide;
cadmium zinc sulphide

emerald green
brominated copper
phthalocyanine; zinc oxide

viridian
hydrated chromium oxide

Prussian green
chlorinated copper
phthalocyanine

burnt sienna
synthetic iron oxide

light red
synthetic iron oxide

raw umber
natural iron oxide

SUGGESTED PALETTES

It is a good idea for beginners to start with a very restricted palette of six colours and use the charts relating to these six colours to develop their colour skills and discover their preferences. They can then augment their palette as they gain experience. A good minimum palette for a beginner is shown here:

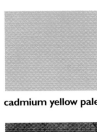

cadmium yellow pale

cadmium scarlet

French ultramarine

burnt sienna

viridian

**violet
(dioxazine)**

One of the most popular supports for works in oil paints is canvas. Canvases are available pre-stretched in various sizes and different textures from smooth to extremely coarse grained.

lemon yellow

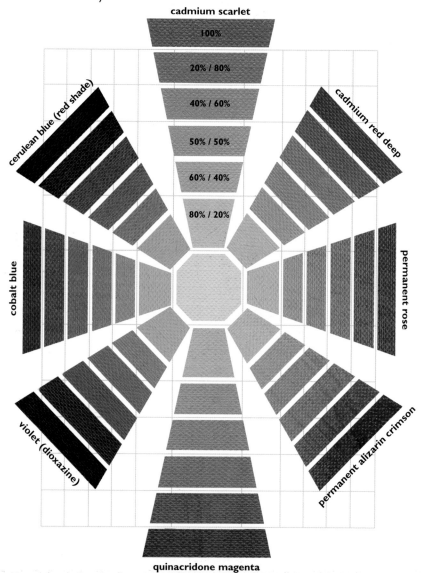

cadmium scarlet

100%

20% / 80%

40% / 60%

50% / 50%

60% / 40%

80% / 20%

cerulean blue (red shade)

cadmium red deep

cobalt blue

permanent rose

violet (dioxazine)

permanent alizarin crimson

quinacridone magenta

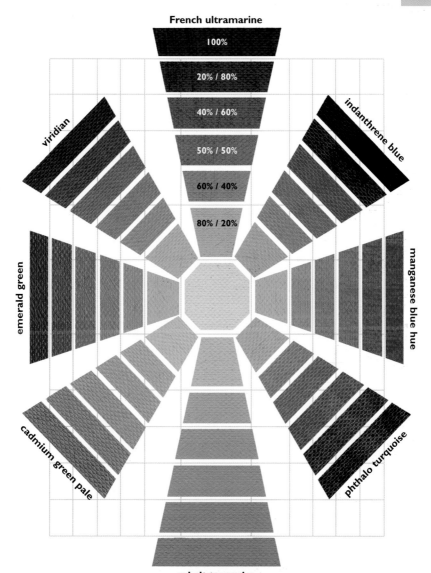

French ultramarine

100%

20% / 80%

40% / 60%

50% / 50%

60% / 40%

80% / 20%

viridian

indanthrene blue

emerald green

manganese blue hue

cadmium green pale

phthalo turquoise

cobalt turquoise

cadmium yellow pale

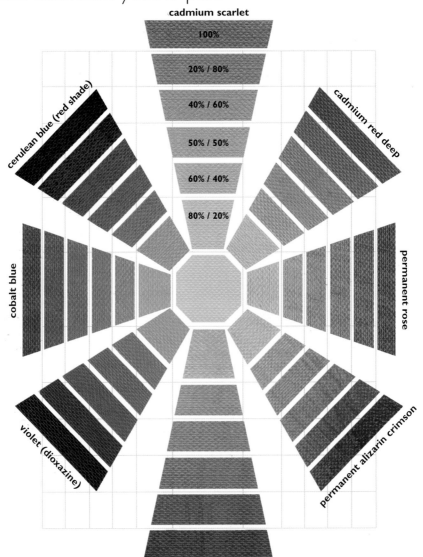

cadmium scarlet

100%

20% / 80%

40% / 60%

50% / 50%

60% / 40%

80% / 20%

cerulean blue (red shade)

cadmium red deep

cobalt blue

permanent rose

violet (dioxazine)

permanent alizarin crimson

quinacridone magenta

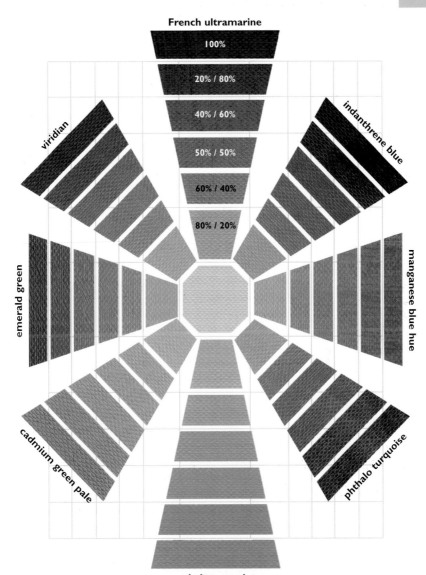

French ultramarine

100%

20% / 80%

40% / 60%

50% / 50%

60% / 40%

80% / 20%

viridian

indanthrene blue

emerald green

manganese blue hue

cadmium green pale

phthalo turquoise

cobalt turquoise

Naples yellow deep

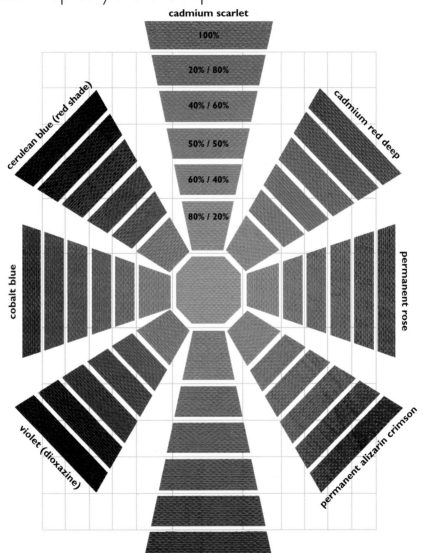

cadmium scarlet

100%

20% / 80%

40% / 60%

50% / 50%

60% / 40%

80% / 20%

cerulean blue (red shade)

cadmium red deep

cobalt blue

permanent rose

violet (dioxazine)

permanent alizarin crimson

quinacridone magenta

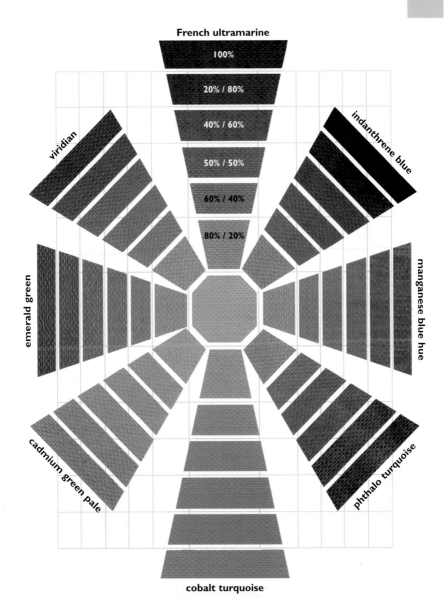

French ultramarine

100%

20% / 80%

40% / 60%

50% / 50%

60% / 40%

80% / 20%

indanthrene blue

viridian

emerald green

manganese blue hue

cadmium green pale

phthalo turquoise

cobalt turquoise

cadmium yellow deep

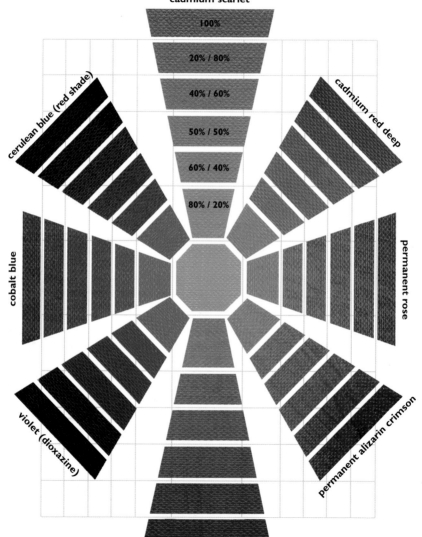

cadmium scarlet

100%

20% / 80%

40% / 60%

50% / 50%

60% / 40%

80% / 20%

cerulean blue (red shade)

cadmium red deep

cobalt blue

permanent rose

violet (dioxazine)

permanent alizarin crimson

quinacridone magenta

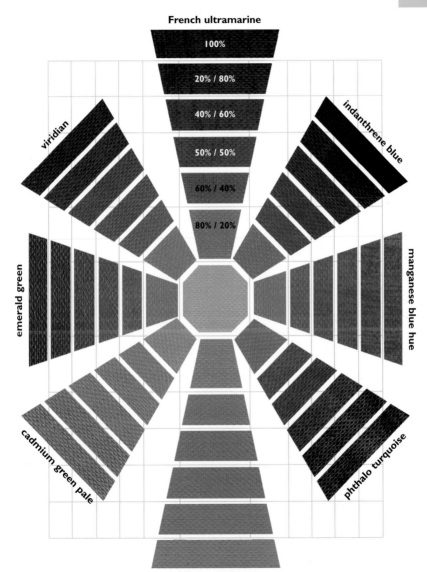

French ultramarine

100%

20% / 80%

40% / 60%

50% / 50%

60% / 40%

80% / 20%

viridian

indanthrene blue

emerald green

manganese blue hue

cadmium green pale

phthalo turquoise

cobalt turquoise

orange

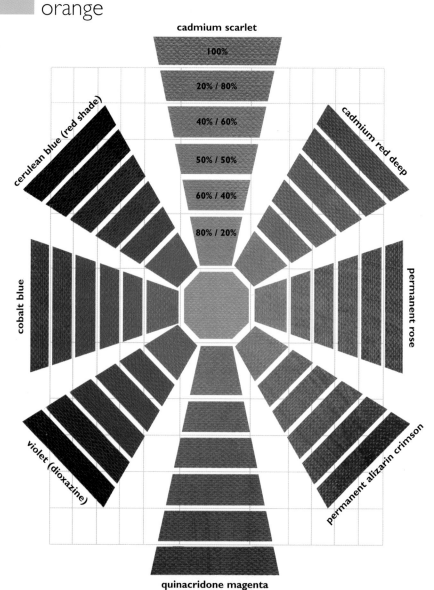

cadmium scarlet

100%

20% / 80%

40% / 60%

50% / 50%

60% / 40%

80% / 20%

cerulean blue (red shade)

cadmium red deep

cobalt blue

permanent rose

violet (dioxazine)

permanent alizarin crimson

quinacridone magenta

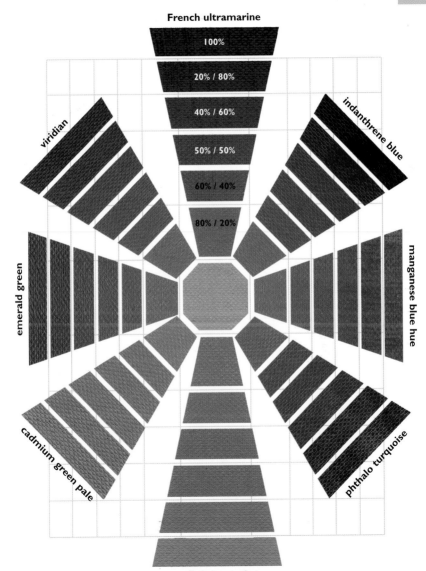

French ultramarine

100%

20% / 80%

40% / 60%

50% / 50%

60% / 40%

80% / 20%

viridian

indanthrene blue

emerald green

manganese blue hue

cadmium green pale

phthalo turquoise

cobalt turquoise

cadmium scarlet

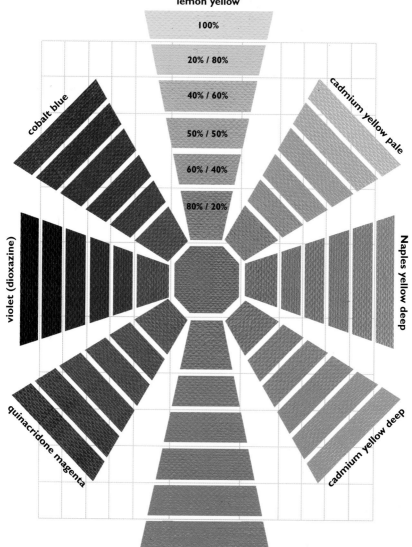

lemon yellow

100%

20% / 80%

40% / 60%

50% / 50%

60% / 40%

80% / 20%

cobalt blue

cadmium yellow pale

violet (dioxazine)

Naples yellow deep

quinacridone magenta

cadmium yellow deep

orange

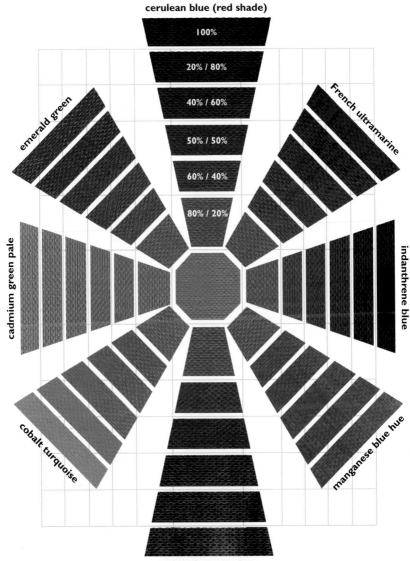

cerulean blue (red shade)

100%

20% / 80%

40% / 60%

50% / 50%

60% / 40%

80% / 20%

emerald green

French ultramarine

cadmium green pale

indanthrene blue

cobalt turquoise

manganese blue hue

phthalo turquoise

cadmium red deep

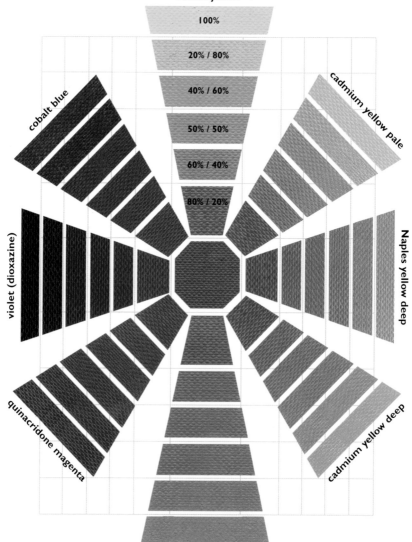

lemon yellow

100%

20% / 80%

40% / 60%

50% / 50%

60% / 40%

80% / 20%

cobalt blue

cadmium yellow pale

violet (dioxazine)

Naples yellow deep

quinacridone magenta

cadmium yellow deep

orange

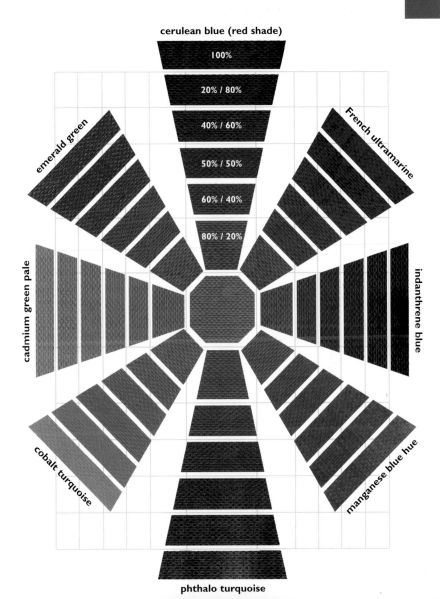

cerulean blue (red shade)

100%

20% / 80%

40% / 60%

50% / 50%

60% / 40%

80% / 20%

emerald green

French ultramarine

cadmium green pale

indanthrene blue

cobalt turquoise

manganese blue hue

phthalo turquoise

permanent rose

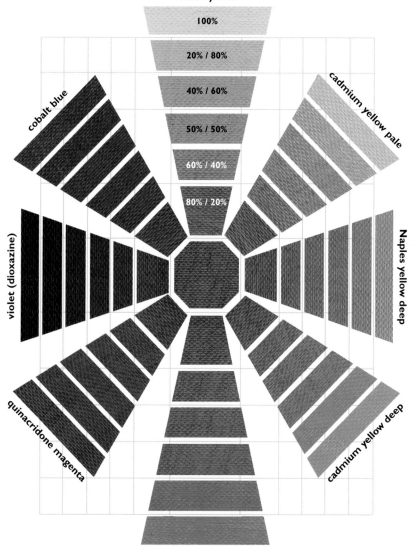

lemon yellow

100%

20% / 80%

40% / 60%

50% / 50%

60% / 40%

80% / 20%

cadmium yellow pale

cobalt blue

Naples yellow deep

violet (dioxazine)

quinacridone magenta

cadmium yellow deep

orange

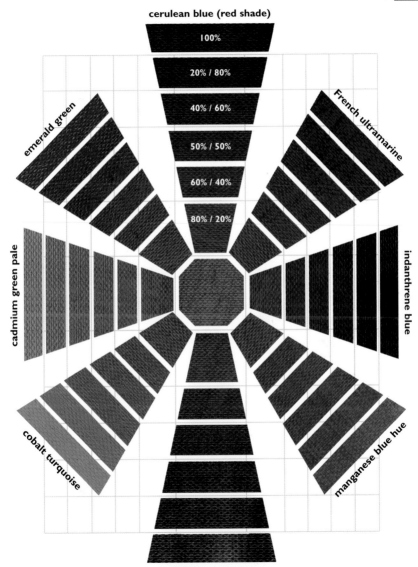

cerulean blue (red shade)

100%

20% / 80%

40% / 60%

50% / 50%

60% / 40%

80% / 20%

emerald green

French ultramarine

cadmium green pale

indanthrene blue

cobalt turquoise

manganese blue hue

phthalo turquoise

permanent alizarin crimson

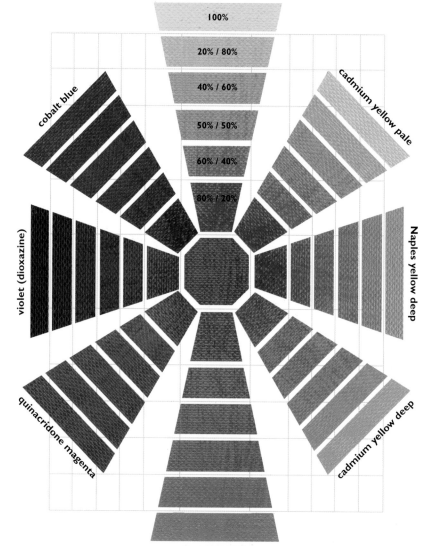

lemon yellow

100%

20% / 80%

40% / 60%

50% / 50%

60% / 40%

80% / 20%

cobalt blue

cadmium yellow pale

violet (dioxazine)

Naples yellow deep

quinacridone magenta

cadmium yellow deep

orange

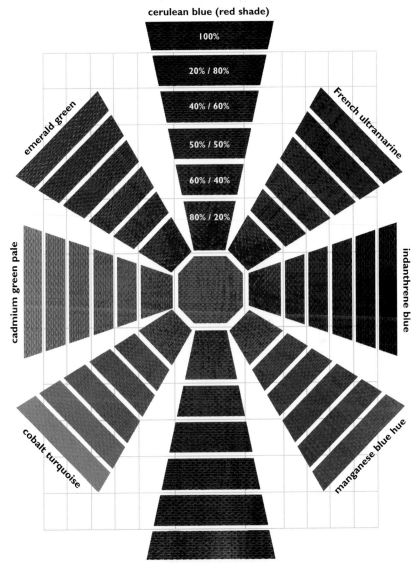

cerulean blue (red shade)

100%

20% / 80%

40% / 60%

50% / 50%

60% / 40%

80% / 20%

emerald green

French ultramarine

cadmium green pale

indanthrene blue

cobalt turquoise

manganese blue hue

phthalo turquoise

quinacridone magenta

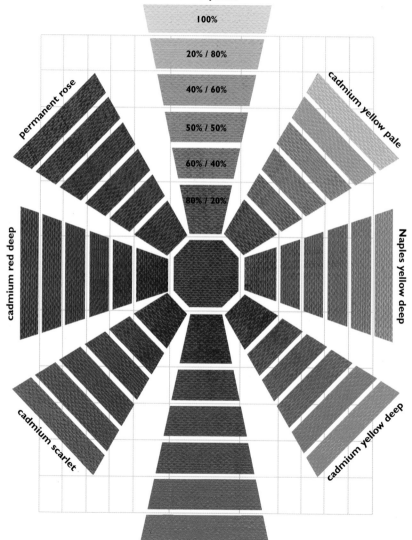

lemon yellow

100%

20% / 80%

40% / 60%

50% / 50%

60% / 40%

80% / 20%

permanent rose

cadmium yellow pale

cadmium red deep

Naples yellow deep

cadmium scarlet

cadmium yellow deep

orange

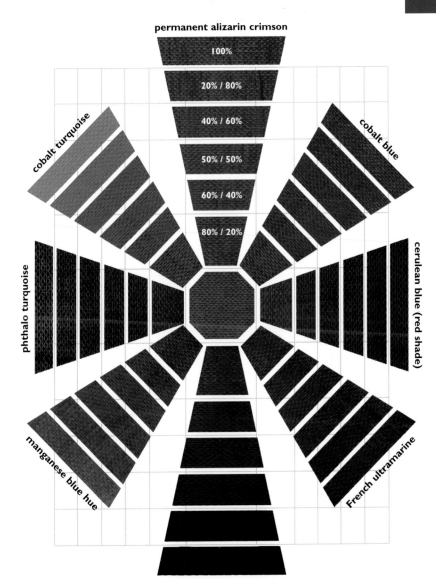

permanent alizarin crimson

100%

20% / 80%

40% / 60%

50% / 50%

60% / 40%

80% / 20%

cobalt turquoise

cobalt blue

phthalo turquoise

cerulean blue (red shade)

manganese blue hue

French ultramarine

indanthrene blue

violet (dioxazine)

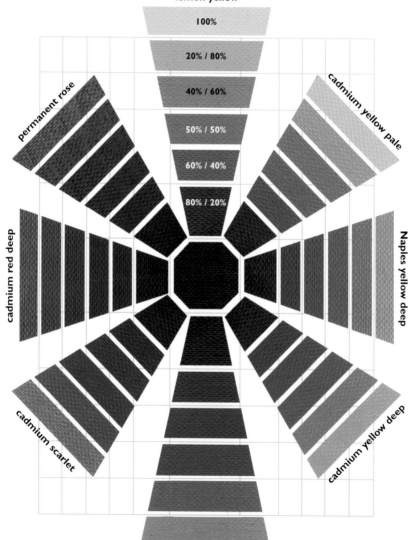

lemon yellow

100%

20% / 80%

40% / 60%

50% / 50%

60% / 40%

80% / 20%

permanent rose

cadmium yellow pale

cadmium red deep

Naples yellow deep

cadmium scarlet

cadmium yellow deep

orange

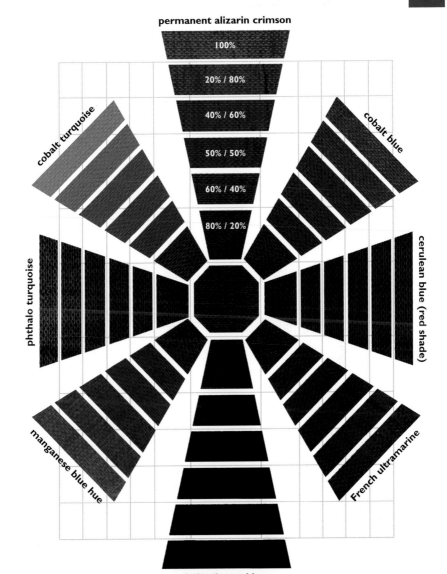

permanent alizarin crimson

100%

20% / 80%

40% / 60%

50% / 50%

60% / 40%

80% / 20%

cobalt turquoise

cobalt blue

phthalo turquoise

cerulean blue (red shade)

manganese blue hue

French ultramarine

indanthrene blue

cobalt blue

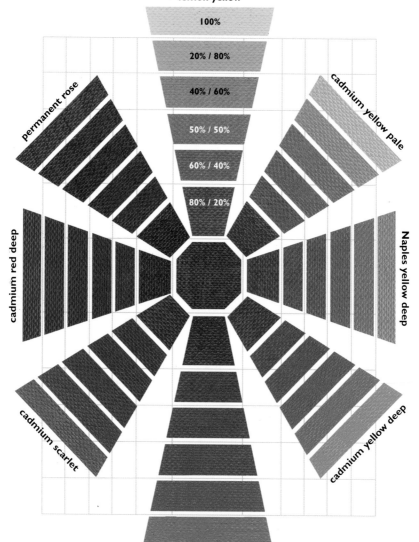

lemon yellow

100%

20% / 80%

40% / 60%

50% / 50%

60% / 40%

80% / 20%

permanent rose

cadmium yellow pale

cadmium red deep

Naples yellow deep

cadmium scarlet

cadmium yellow deep

orange

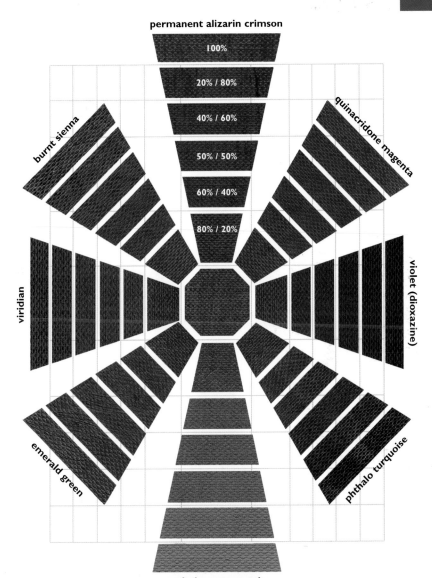

permanent alizarin crimson

100%

20% / 80%

40% / 60%

50% / 50%

60% / 40%

80% / 20%

burnt sienna

quinacridone magenta

viridian

violet (dioxazine)

emerald green

phthalo turquoise

cadmium green pale

cerulean blue (red shade)

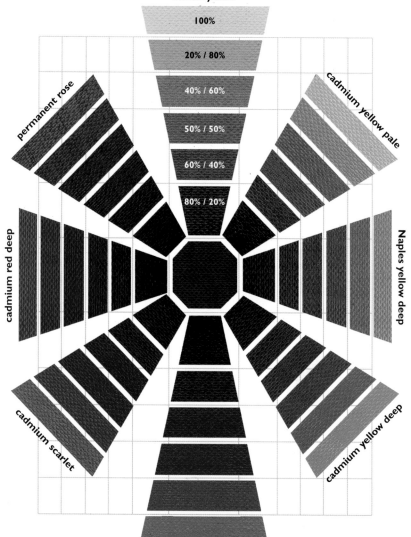

lemon yellow

100%

20% / 80%

40% / 60%

50% / 50%

60% / 40%

80% / 20%

permanent rose

cadmium yellow pale

cadmium red deep

Naples yellow deep

cadmium scarlet

cadmium yellow deep

orange

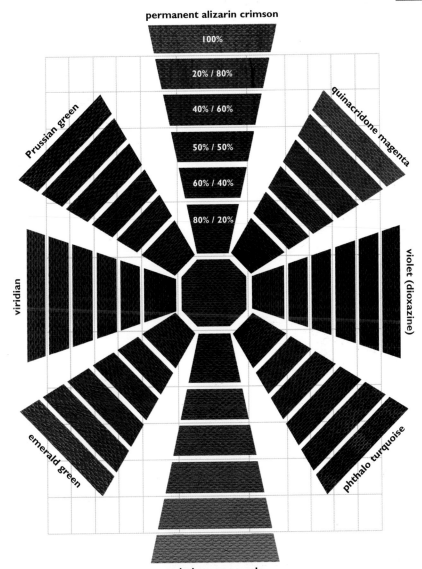

permanent alizarin crimson

100%

20% / 80%

40% / 60%

50% / 50%

60% / 40%

80% / 20%

Prussian green

quinacridone magenta

viridian

violet (dioxazine)

emerald green

phthalo turquoise

cadmium green pale

French ultramarine

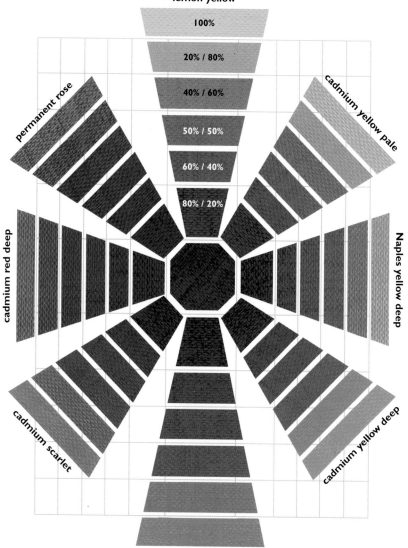

lemon yellow

100%

20% / 80%

40% / 60%

50% / 50%

60% / 40%

80% / 20%

permanent rose

cadmium yellow pale

cadmium red deep

Naples yellow deep

cadmium scarlet

cadmium yellow deep

orange

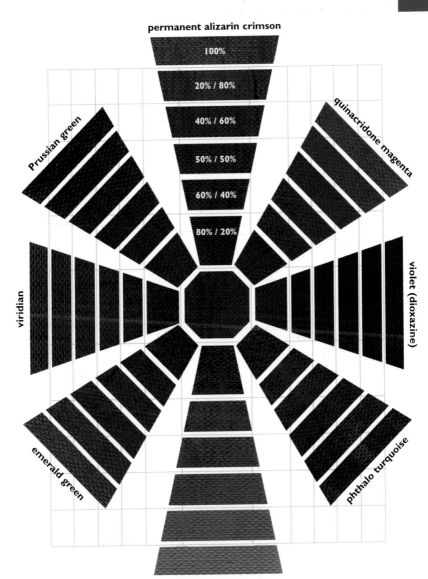

permanent alizarin crimson

100%

20% / 80%

40% / 60%

50% / 50%

60% / 40%

80% / 20%

Prussian green

quinacridone magenta

viridian

violet (dioxazine)

emerald green

phthalo turquoise

cadmium green pale

indanthrene blue

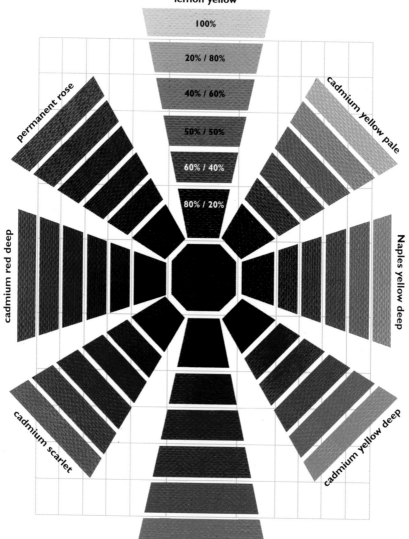

lemon yellow

100%

20% / 80%

40% / 60%

50% / 50%

60% / 40%

80% / 20%

permanent rose

cadmium yellow pale

cadmium red deep

Naples yellow deep

cadmium scarlet

cadmium yellow deep

orange

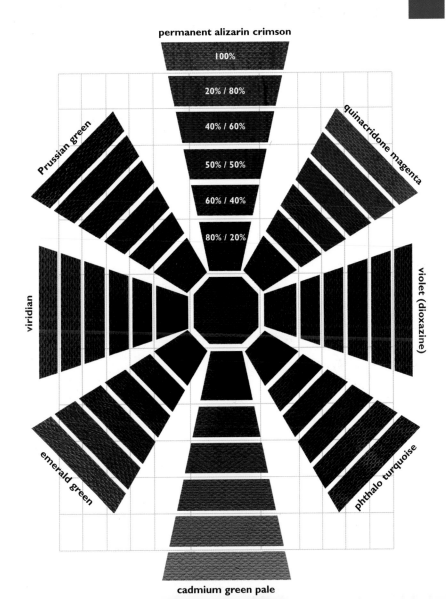

permanent alizarin crimson

100%

20% / 80%

40% / 60%

50% / 50%

60% / 40%

80% / 20%

Prussian green

quinacridone magenta

viridian

violet (dioxazine)

emerald green

phthalo turquoise

cadmium green pale

manganese blue hue

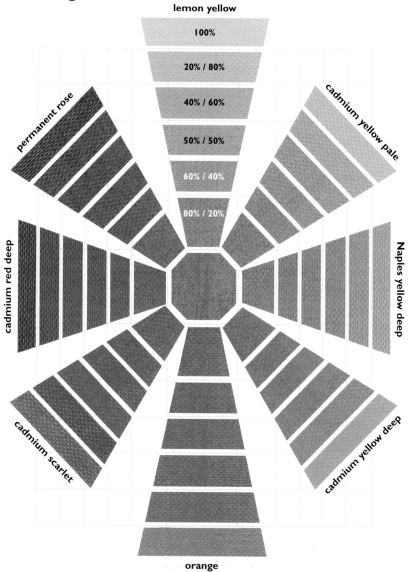

lemon yellow

100%

20% / 80%

40% / 60%

50% / 50%

60% / 40%

80% / 20%

permanent rose

cadmium yellow pale

cadmium red deep

Naples yellow deep

cadmium scarlet

cadmium yellow deep

orange

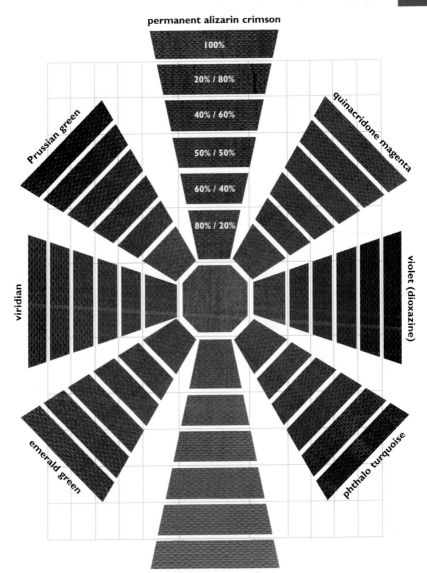

permanent alizarin crimson

100%

20% / 80%

40% / 60%

50% / 50%

60% / 40%

80% / 20%

Prussian green

quinacridone magenta

viridian

violet (dioxazine)

emerald green

phthalo turquoise

cadmium green pale

phthalo turquoise

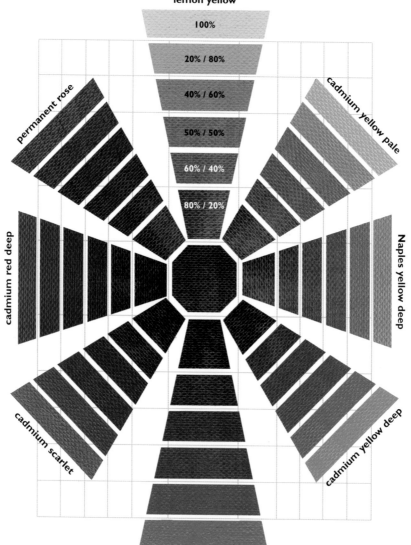

lemon yellow

100%

20% / 80%

40% / 60%

50% / 50%

60% / 40%

80% / 20%

permanent rose

cadmium yellow pale

cadmium red deep

Naples yellow deep

cadmium scarlet

cadmium yellow deep

orange

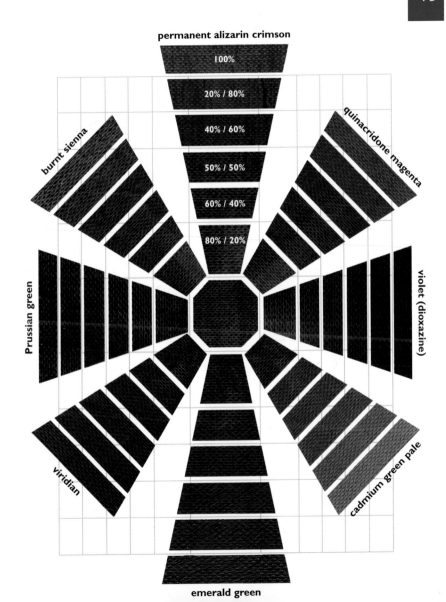

permanent alizarin crimson

100%

20% / 80%

40% / 60%

50% / 50%

60% / 40%

80% / 20%

quinacridone magenta

burnt sienna

violet (dioxazine)

Prussian green

viridian

cadmium green pale

emerald green

cobalt turquoise

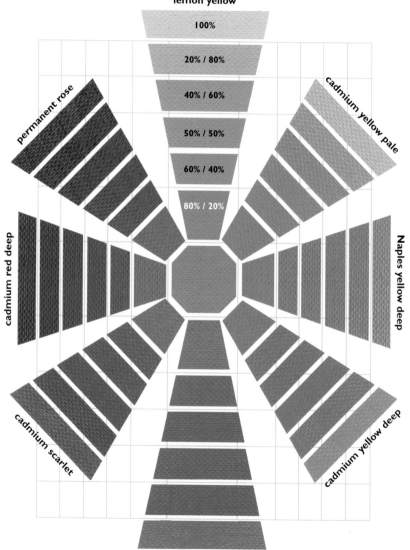

lemon yellow

100%

20% / 80%

40% / 60%

50% / 50%

60% / 40%

80% / 20%

permanent rose

cadmium yellow pale

cadmium red deep

Naples yellow deep

cadmium scarlet

cadmium yellow deep

orange

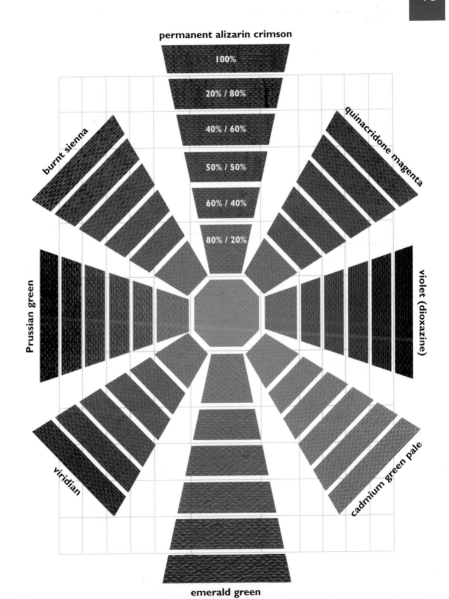

permanent alizarin crimson

100%

20% / 80%

40% / 60%

50% / 50%

60% / 40%

80% / 20%

burnt sienna

quinacridone magenta

Prussian green

violet (dioxazine)

viridian

cadmium green pale

emerald green

cadmium green pale

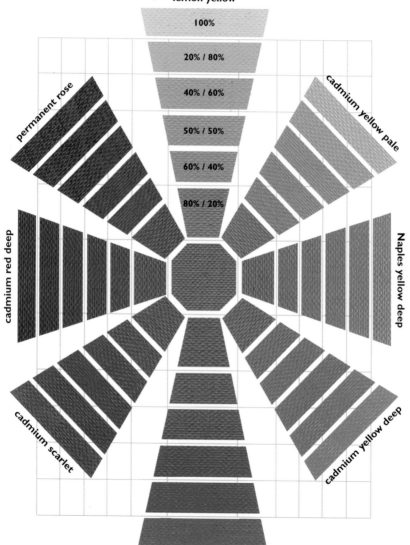

lemon yellow

100%

20% / 80%

40% / 60%

50% / 50%

60% / 40%

80% / 20%

permanent rose

cadmium yellow pale

cadmium red deep

Naples yellow deep

cadmium scarlet

cadmium yellow deep

orange

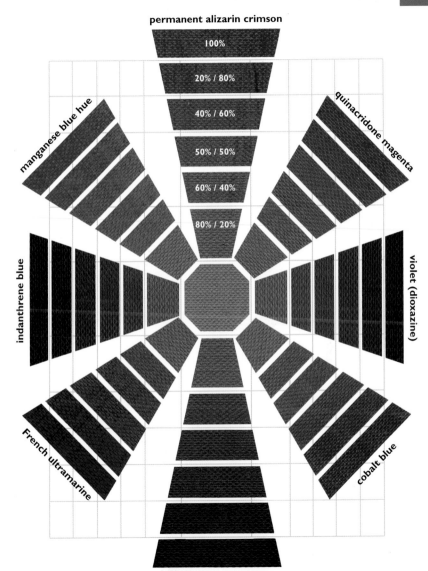

permanent alizarin crimson

100%

20% / 80%

40% / 60%

50% / 50%

60% / 40%

80% / 20%

manganese blue hue

quinacridone magenta

indanthrene blue

violet (dioxazine)

French ultramarine

cobalt blue

cerulean blue (red shade)

emerald green

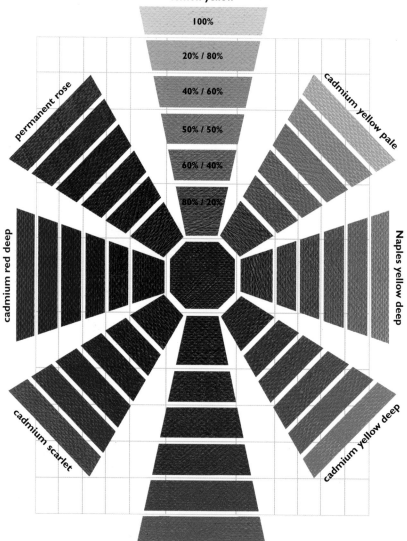

lemon yellow

100%

20% / 80%

40% / 60%

50% / 50%

60% / 40%

80% / 20%

permanent rose

cadmium yellow pale

cadmium red deep

Naples yellow deep

cadmium scarlet

cadmium yellow deep

orange

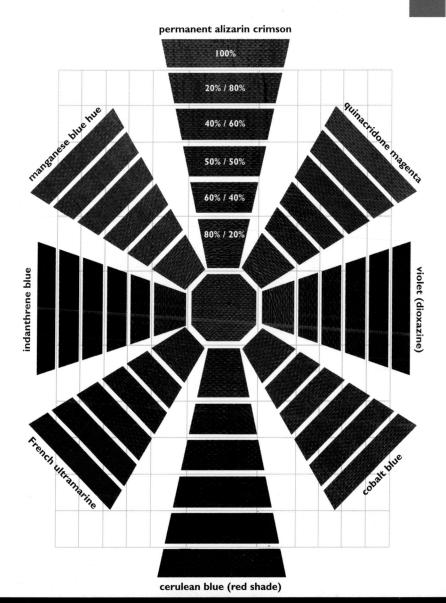

permanent alizarin crimson

100%

20% / 80%

40% / 60%

50% / 50%

60% / 40%

80% / 20%

manganese blue hue

quinacridone magenta

indanthrene blue

violet (dioxazine)

French ultramarine

cobalt blue

cerulean blue (red shade)

more brown ▸▸ ▸▸ ▸▸

viridian

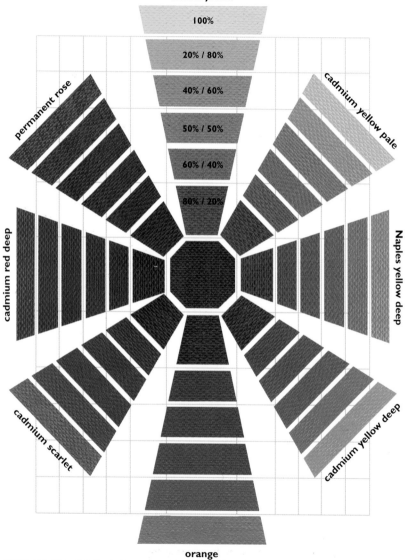

lemon yellow

100%

20% / 80%

40% / 60%

50% / 50%

60% / 40%

80% / 20%

cadmium yellow pale

permanent rose

Naples yellow deep

cadmium red deep

cadmium yellow deep

cadmium scarlet

orange

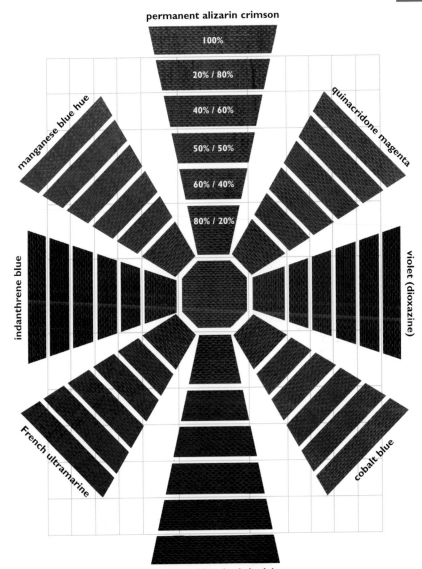

permanent alizarin crimson

100%

20% / 80%

40% / 60%

50% / 50%

60% / 40%

80% / 20%

manganese blue hue

quinacridone magenta

indanthrene blue

violet (dioxazine)

French ultramarine

cobalt blue

cerulean blue (red shade)

Prussian green

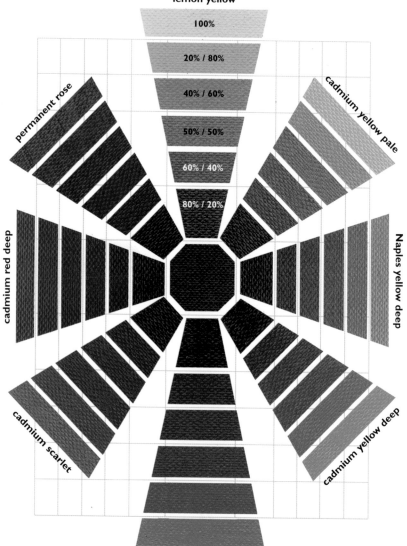

lemon yellow

100%

20% / 80%

40% / 60%

50% / 50%

60% / 40%

80% / 20%

permanent rose

cadmium yellow pale

cadmium red deep

Naples yellow deep

cadmium scarlet

cadmium yellow deep

orange

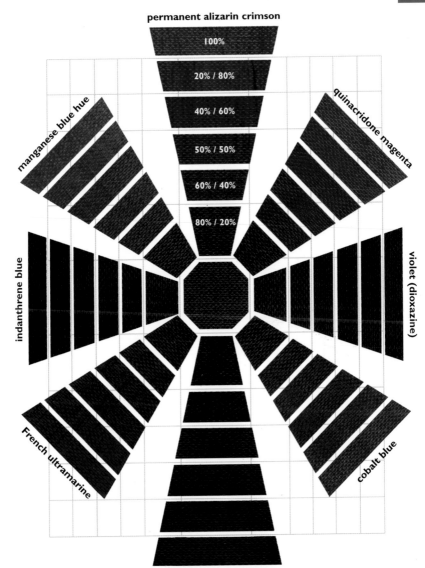

permanent alizarin crimson

100%

20% / 80%

40% / 60%

50% / 50%

60% / 40%

80% / 20%

manganese blue hue

quinacridone magenta

indanthrene blue

violet (dioxazine)

French ultramarine

cobalt blue

cerulean blue (red shade)

burnt sienna

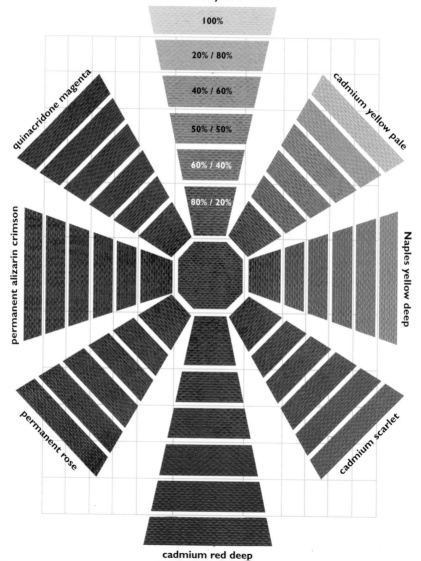

lemon yellow

100%

20% / 80%

40% / 60%

50% / 50%

60% / 40%

80% / 20%

quinacridone magenta

cadmium yellow pale

permanent alizarin crimson

Naples yellow deep

permanent rose

cadmium scarlet

cadmium red deep

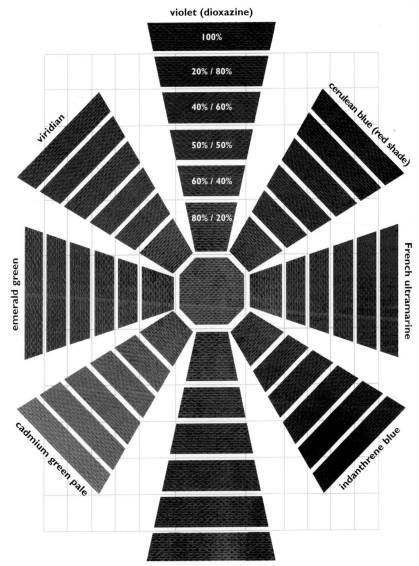

violet (dioxazine)

100%

20% / 80%

40% / 60%

50% / 50%

60% / 40%

80% / 20%

viridian

cerulean blue (red shade)

emerald green

French ultramarine

cadmium green pale

indanthrene blue

phthalo turquoise

light red

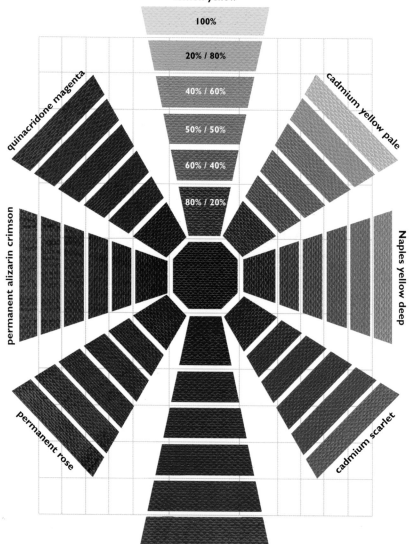

lemon yellow

100%

20% / 80%

40% / 60%

50% / 50%

60% / 40%

80% / 20%

quinacridone magenta

cadmium yellow pale

permanent alizarin crimson

Naples yellow deep

permanent rose

cadmium scarlet

cadmium red deep

◀◀ ◀◀ ◀◀ more green

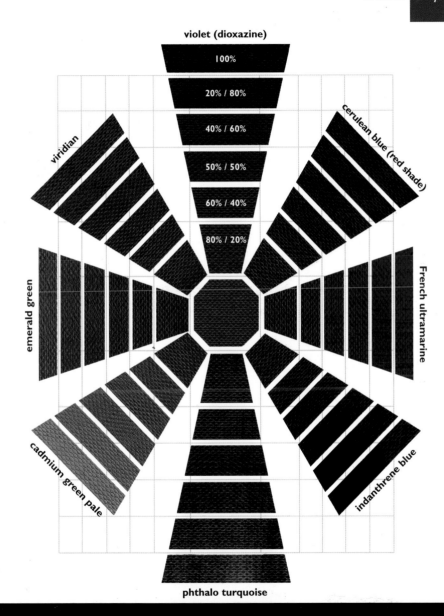

violet (dioxazine)

100%

20% / 80%

40% / 60%

50% / 50%

60% / 40%

80% / 20%

cerulean blue (red shade)

viridian

French ultramarine

emerald green

indanthrene blue

cadmium green pale

phthalo turquoise

raw umber

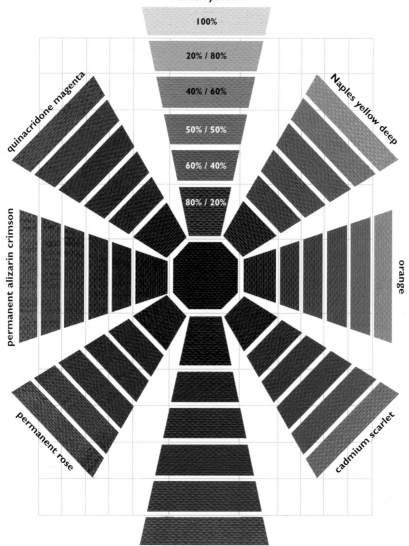

lemon yellow

100%

20% / 80%

40% / 60%

50% / 50%

60% / 40%

80% / 20%

quinacridone magenta

Naples yellow deep

permanent alizarin crimson

orange

permanent rose

cadmium scarlet

cadmium red deep

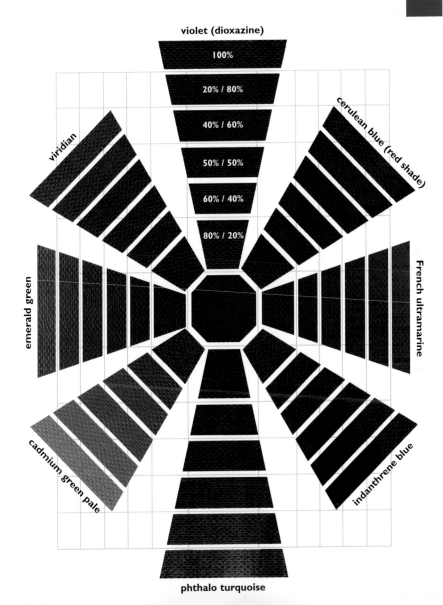

violet (dioxazine)

100%

20% / 80%

40% / 60%

50% / 50%

60% / 40%

80% / 20%

viridian

cerulean blue (red shade)

emerald green

French ultramarine

cadmium green pale

indanthrene blue

phthalo turquoise

index

index

acknowledgements

Photographs on pp. 1, 2, 3, 24, 27, 80–81, 83, 136–137, 139 © Winsor & Newton